ADVANCED MANUFACTURING PROCESSES

AUTHOR (S)

Dr. Ranjeet Kumar Sahu
Assistant Professor (Grade 1)
Department of Mechanical Engineering
National Institute of Technology
Karnataka, Surathkal

Mr. Devendra Laxman Kamble
Research Scholar
Department of Mechanical Engineering
National Institute of Technology
Karnataka, Surathkal

REVIEWER

Dr. S. Dhanalakshmi
HOD/Mechanical Engineering
Government Polytechnic College, Painkinar Village,
Cheyyar, Tamil Nadu- 604407

KHANNA BOOK PUBLISHING CO. (P) Ltd.
4C/4344, Ansari Road, Darya Ganj,
New Delhi, India

All India Council for Technical Education
Nelson Mandela Marg, Vasant Kunj,
New Delhi, India

Dear Readers,

To prevent the piracy, this book is secured with HIGH SECURITY HOLOGRAM on the front title cover. In case you don't find the hologram on the front cover title, please write us to at contact@khannabooks.com or whatsapp us at +91-99109 09320 and avail special gift voucher for yourself.

Specimen of Hologram on front Cover title:

Moreover, there is a SPECIAL DISCOUNT COUPON for you with EVERY HOLOGRAM.

How to avail this SPECIAL DISCOUNT:

Step 1: Scratch the hologram

Step 2: Under the scratch area, your "coupon code" is available

Step 3: Logon to www.khannabooks.com

Step 4: Use your "coupon code" in the shopping cart and get your copy at a special discount

Step 5: Enjoy your reading!

ISBN: 978-93-5538-556-7

Book Code: DIP498EN

Advanced Manufacturing Processes

by Dr. Ranjeet Kumar Sahu and
Mr. Devendra Laxman Kamble

First Edition: 2026

Originally Published by:
All India Council for Technical Education, Ministry of Education, GOI

Exclusively Published & Distributed by:
Khanna Book Publishing Co. (P) Ltd.
4C/4344, Ansari Road, Daryaganj,
New Delhi (INDIA)

Visit us at: **www.khannabooks.com**
Write us at: **contact@khannabooks.com**

To view complete list of books, Please scan the QR Code: KPH

Printed in Bharat.

प्रो. टी. जी. सीताराम
अध्यक्ष
Prof. T. G. Sitharam
Chairman

सत्यमेव जयते

आज़ादी का अमृत महोत्सव

अखिल भारतीय तकनीकी शिक्षा परिषद्
(भारत सरकार का एक सांविधिक निकाय)
(शिक्षा मंत्रालय, भारत सरकार)
नेल्सन मंडेला मार्ग, वसंत कुंज, नई दिल्ली-110070
दूरभाष : 011-26131498
ई-मेल : chairman@aicte-india.org

ALL INDIA COUNCIL FOR TECHNICAL EDUCATION
(A STATUTORY BODY OF THE GOVT. OF INDIA)
(Ministry of Education, Govt. of India)
Nelson Mandela Marg, Vasant Kunj, New Delhi-110070
Phone : 011-26131498
E-mail : chairman@aicte-india.org

FOREWORD

Engineers are the backbone of any modern society. They are the ones responsible for the marvels as well as the improved quality of life across the world. Engineers have driven humanity towards greater heights in a more evolved and unprecedented manner.

The All India Council for Technical Education (AICTE), have spared no efforts towards the strengthening of the technical education in the country. AICTE is always committed towards promoting quality Technical Education to make India a modern developed nation emphasizing on the overall welfare of mankind.

An array of initiatives has been taken by AICTE in last decade which have been accelerated now by the National Education Policy (NEP) 2020. The implementation of NEP under the visionary leadership of Hon'ble Prime Minister of India envisages the provision for education in regional languages to all, thereby ensuring that every graduate becomes competent enough and is in a position to contribute towards the national growth and development through innovation & entrepreneurship.

One of the spheres where AICTE had been relentlessly working since past couple of years is providing high quality original technical contents at Under Graduate & Diploma level prepared and translated by eminent educators in various Indian languages to its aspirants. For students pursuing 2nd year of their Engineering education, AICTE has identified 87 books, which shall be translated into 12 Indian languages - Hindi, Tamil, Gujarati, Odia, Bengali, Kannada, Urdu, Punjabi, Telugu, Marathi, Assamese & Malayalam. In addition to the English medium, books in different Indian Languages are going to support the students to understand the concepts in their respective mother tongue.

On behalf of AICTE, I express sincere gratitude to all distinguished authors, reviewers and translators from the renowned institutions of high repute for their admirable contribution in a record span of time.

AICTE is confident that these outcomes based original contents shall help aspirants to master the subject with comprehension and greater ease.

(Prof. T. G. Sitharam)

ACKNOWLEDGEMENT

The authors are grateful to the authorities of AICTE, particularly Prof. (Dr.) T G Sitharam, Chairman; Dr. Abhay Jere, Vice-Chairman; Prof. Rajiv Kumar, Member-Secretary; Dr. Sunil Luthra, Director and Reena Sharma, Hindi Officer Training and Learning Bureau for their planning to publish the books on Building Electrification. We sincerely acknowledge the valuable contributions of the reviewer of the book Dr. S. Dhanalakshmi, HOD/Mechanical Engineering, Government Polytechnic College, Cheyyar, Tamil Nadu.

The authors would like to thank PhD student Mr. Tejanshu Sekar Sahu for their valuable support in completing this book.

First and foremost, we thank our parents and families for their unwavering support, patience, and encouragement, which gave us the strength and motivation to complete this project. Their belief in us has been our greatest inspiration.

This book is an outcome of various suggestions of AICTE members, experts, and authors who shared their opinions and thoughts to further develop engineering education in our country. Acknowledgments are due to the contributors and different workers in this field whose published books, review articles, papers, photographs, footnotes, references, and other valuable information enriched us at the time of writing the book.

Dr. Ranjeet Kumar Sahu
Mr. Devendra Laxman Kamble

PREFACE

The field of Advanced Manufacturing Techniques represents a transformative era in industrial production, where innovation, precision, and efficiency converge to redefine the possibilities of manufacturing. As global industries evolve, the demand for more sophisticated, adaptable, and sustainable manufacturing methods has never been greater. Advanced manufacturing techniques are at the heart of this evolution, enabling the creation of complex geometries, the integration of new materials, and the optimization of production processes in ways that were once unimaginable. This book aims to provide a comprehensive overview of the latest advancements in advanced manufacturing techniques, offering insights into both the fundamental principles and practical applications that are driving this field forward. It covers a wide range of topics, including Jigs and Fixtures, Jig boring and plastic processing, Modern machining process, CNC milling machines and machine tool automation, Special purpose machines, and maintenance of machine tools in modern production environments. By exploring these cutting-edge techniques, the book underscores how they contribute to improving product quality, reducing waste, and enhancing the overall efficiency of manufacturing processes. Whether you are a student, researcher, engineer, or industry professional, this book is designed to serve as a valuable resource, offering both theoretical knowledge and practical guidance. It is our hope that the insights presented here will inspire further innovation and contribute to the ongoing advancement of manufacturing techniques, ultimately shaping the future of how products are designed, produced, and delivered.

Dr. Ranjeet Kumar Sahu

Mr. Devendra Laxman Kamble

OUTCOME BASED EDUCATION

For the implementation of an outcome-based education the first requirement is to develop an outcome-based curriculum and incorporate an outcome-based assessment in the education system. By going through outcome-based assessments evaluators will be able to evaluate whether the students have achieved the outlined standard, specific and measurable outcomes. With the proper incorporation of outcome-based education there will be a definite commitment to achieve a minimum standard for all learners without giving up at any level. At the end of the programme running with the aid of outcome-based education, a student will be able to arrive at the following outcomes:

PO1. **Basic and Discipline specific knowledge:** Apply knowledge of basic mathematics, science and engineering fundamentals and engineering specialization to solve the engineering problems.

PO2. **Problem analysis:** Identify and analyses well-defined engineering problems using codified standard methods.

PO3. **Design/development of solutions:** Design solutions for well-defined technical problems and assist with the design of systems components or processes to meet specified needs.

PO4. **Engineering Tools, Experimentation and Testing:** Apply modern engineering tools and appropriate technique to conduct standard tests and measurements.

PO5. **Engineering practices for society, sustainability, and environment:** Apply appropriate technology in context of society, sustainability, environment, and ethical practices.

PO6. **Project Management:** Use engineering management principles individually, as a team member or a leader to manage projects and effectively communicate about well-defined engineering activities.

PO7. **Life-long learning:** Ability to analyse individual needs and engage in updating in the context of technological changes.

COURSE OUTCOMES

After completion of the course the students will be able to:

CO-1: Know the Operation and control of different advanced machine tools and equipments.

CO-2: Produce jobs as per specified requirements by selecting the specific machining process.

CO-3: Develop the mind set for modern trends in manufacturing and automation.

CO-4: Identify the different fabrication methods viz., sheet forming, blow moulding, laminating

CO-5: Know different non-traditional machining processes, CNC milling machines, special purpose machines.

CO-6: Work as maintenance engineer.

Mapping of Course Outcomes with Programme Outcomes to be done according to the matrix given below:

Course Outcomes	Expected Mapping with Programme Outcomes *(1-Weak Correlation; 2- Medium correlation; 3- Strong Correlation)*						
	PO-1	**PO-2**	**PO-3**	**PO-4**	**PO-5**	**PO-6**	**PO-7**
CO-1	1	2	2	3	2	3	3
CO-2	1	2	3	2	2	3	3
CO-3	3	2	3	1	1	2	3
CO-4	2	3	3	2	1	1	2
CO-5	2	2	3	1	2	2	3
CO-6	2	3	2	2	1	2	3

GUIDELINES FOR TEACHERS

To implement Outcome Based Education (OBE) knowledge level and skill set of the students should be enhanced. Teachers should take major responsibility for the proper implementation of OBE. Some of the responsibilities (not limited to) for the teachers in OBE system may be as follows:

- Within reasonable constraint, they should manoeuvre time to the best advantage of all students.
- They should assess the students only upon certain defined criterion without considering any other potential ineligibility to discriminate them.
- They should try to grow the learning abilities of the students to a certain level before they leave the institute.
- They should try to ensure that all the students are equipped with the quality knowledge as well as competence after they finish their education.
- They should always encourage the students to develop their ultimate performance capabilities.
- They should facilitate and encourage group work and team work to consolidate newer approach.
- They should follow Bloom's taxonomy in every part of the assessment.

Bloom's Taxonomy

Level	Teacher should Check	Student should be able to	Possible Mode of Assessment
Create	Students ability to create	Design or Create	Mini project
Evaluate	Students ability to justify	Argue or Defend	Assignment
Analyse	Students ability to distinguish	Differentiate or Distinguish	Project/Lab Methodology
Apply	Students ability to use information	Operate or Demonstrate	Technical Presentation/ Demonstration
Understand	Students ability to explain the ideas	Explain or Classify	Presentation/Seminar
Remember	Students ability to recall (or remember)	Define or Recall	Quiz

GUIDELINES FOR STUDENTS

Students should take equal responsibility for implementing the OBE. Some of the responsibilities (not limited to) for the students in OBE system are as follows:

- Students should be aware of each UO before the start of a unit in each course.
- Students should be aware of each CO before the start of the course.
- Students should be aware of each PO before the start of the programme.
- Students should think critically and reasonably with proper reflection and action.
- Learning of the students should be connected and integrated with practical and real-life consequences.
- Students should be aware of their competency at every level of OBE.

LIST OF ABBREVIATIONS

Abbreviations	Full form
C.I	Cast iron
PVC	Polyvinyl chloride
ABC plastics	Acrylobutadiene styrene
PTFE	Polytetrafluory ethylene
EDM	Electrical discharge machining
USM	Ultrasonic machining
WEDM	Wire cut EDM
LBM	Laser beam machining
ECM	Electrochemical machining
AJM	Abrasive jet machining
WJM	Water jet machining
AWJM	Abrasive water jet machining
IBM	Ion beam machining
PAM	Plasma arc machining
CHM	Chemical Machining
MRR	Material Removal Rate
WC	Tungsten carbide
Cu	Copper
Al	Aluminium
Gr	Graphite
Au	Gold
Ag	Silver
DI	De-ionized
DC	Direct current
RC	Resistance-Capacitance
FET	Field Effect transistor
TWR	Tool wear rate
OC	Overcut
μs	Microseconds
IP	Peak current

Al_2O_3	Aluminium oxide
SiC	Silicon carbide
HAZ	Heat-affected zone
PLC	Programming logic control PLC
CNC	Computer numerical control
VMC	Vertical machining center
HMC	Horizontal machining center
ATC	Automatic tool changer
APC	Automatic pallet changer
NC	Numeric control
CAPP	Computer-Aided Part Programming
CAD	Computer-Aided Design
ERP	Enterprise Resource Planning
MES	Manufacturing Execution Systems
CPU	Central processing unit
FBD	Function Block Diagram
ST	Structured Text
SFC	Sequential Function Chart
HMI	Human-Machine Interfaces
SCADA	Supervisory Control and Data Acquisition
RAM	Random access memory
ROM	Read only memory
HHT	Handheld terminals
SPM	Special purpose machine
TPM	Total productive maintenance
KPI	Key performance indicators
MTBF	Mean time between failures
MTTR	Mean time to repair
OEE	Overall equipment effectiveness
AM	Autonomous maintenance
PM	Planned maintenance
QM	Quality maintenance
EEM	Early equipment management

LIST OF SYMBOLS

Symbol	Description
N/mm^2	Pressure
^0C	Degree Celsius
T_{on}	Pulse On time
T_{off}	Pulse Off time
D	Duty cycle
f	Frequency
$W1$	weight of the workpiece before machining.
$W2$	weight of the workpiece after machining
ρ	Density of workpiece
Wt_1	weight of the tool before machining
Wt_2	weight of the tool after machining
t	Machining time
D_h	Diameter of the hole machined in the workpiece
Wt_2	Diameter of the tool
m/min	Meter/minute
L	Distance between lower and upper guide

LIST OF FIGURES

Sr. No.	Name of Figure	Page. No.
1.1	Leaf jig	3
1.2	Box Jig	4
1.3	Template Jig	4
1.4	Plate Jig	5
1.5	Indexing jig	5
1.6	Principle of Location	6
1.7	Cylindrical Locator	8
1.8	Fixed V-locator	8
1.9	Adjustable V-locator	9
1.1	Plain bush	9
1.11	Headed Bush	10
1.12	Long bush in two sections	10
1.13	Vice fixture	11
1.14	(a) Vertical milling machine (b) Setting block (c) Tenon	13
1.15	Boring fixture	14
1.16	Grinding fixture	15
1.17	Strap clamp	17
1.18	Direct pressure cam operated clamp	17
1.19	Screw clamp	18
1.20	Wedge clamp	19
1.21	Toggle clamp	19
1.22	Hydraulic clamp	20
1.23	Pneumatic clamp	21
2.1	Photo of Jig boring machine	25
2.2	Single column jig boring machine	26
2.3	Double column jig boring machine	27
2.4	(a) Thermoplastic plastic (b) Thermosetting plastic	30
2.5	Injection Moulding (Ram type)	32
2.6	Injection Moulding (Screw type)	32
2.7	Compression moulding	33-34
2.8	Types of compression moulding	35
2.9	Transfer moulding	36

2.10	Extrusion of plastic	37
2.11	Calendering	38
2.12	Direct blow moulding	38
2.13	Indirect moulding	39
2.14	Manufacture of laminated sheets	40
2.15	Manufacture of tubes and rods	41
3.1	Schematic of ultrasonic machining	48
3.2	Schematic representation of EDM	50
3.3	Voltage and current characteristics waveform	51
3.4	Material removal mechanism in EDM	52
3.5	Components of EDM	53
3.6	RC relaxation-type pulse generator	54
3.7	Transistor-type pulse generator	55
3.8	(a) Overcut (b) Taper cut	58
3.9	Wire EDM equipment	59
3.10	Schematic diagram of wire EDM	60
3.11	Schematic illustration of the distance between the wire guides	62
3.12	AWJ cutting head	64
3.13	Schematic of the AWJM process	65
3.14	Hydraulic pump	66
3.15	Hydraulic pressure intensifier	66
3.16	Accumulator unit	67
3.17	Tubing	67
3.18	Guide nozzle	67
3.19	Nozzle mechanism	68
3.20	Catcher tank	68
3.21	Schematic of laser beam machining	70
3.22	Schematic of ECM	71
4.1	Vertical machining center	78
4.2	Horizontal machining center	79
4.3	Point-to-point based control system	80
4.4	Straight-cut system	81
4.5	Contouring path control system	81
4.6	Absolute system	82

4.7	Incremental system	82
4.8	NC-based controller system	83
4.9	CNC controller	83
4.10	Canned boring cycle	88
4.11	Open loop system	99
4.12	Closed-loop system	99
4.13	Block diagram of PLC	101

LIST OF TABLES

Table. no	Title	Page. No.
3.1	Comparison between traditional and modern machining processes	46
3.2	Classification of Non-traditional machining process	47
4.1	Movement of axes	78
4.2	G-codes	83
4.3	M-codes	86

TABLE OF CONTENT

Foreword		iii
Acknowledgment		iv
Preface		v
Outcome Based Education		vi
Course Outcomes		vii
Guidelines for Teachers		viii
Guidelines for Students		ix
List of Abbreviations		x
List of Symbols		xii
List of Figures		xiii
List of Tables		xvi
Unit 1: Jigs and Fixtures		**1-22**
Unit specifics		1
Rationale		1
Pre-requisites		2
Unit outcomes		2
Introduction		2
1.1	Jig	2
1.2	Types of Jig	3
	1.2.1 Leaf Jig	3
	1.2.2 Box jig	3
	1.2.3 Template jig	4
	1.2.4 Plate Jig	4
	1.2.5 Indexing Jig	5
	1.2.6 Universal jig	5
1.3	Basic principle of location	5
1.4	Drill Bushes	9
	1.4.1 Plain Bush	9
	1.4.2 Headed bushes	9
	1.4.3 Long bush in two sections	10
1.5	Vice Fixture	10
1.6	Milling Fixtures	11

1.7 Boring Fixture 14
1.8 Grinding Fixtures 14
1.9 Important considerations in clamp design 15
1.9.1 Type of Clamps 16
Know More 21
Summary 21
Exercise 21
References 22

Unit 2: Jig Boring and Plastic Processing **23-43**
Unit specifics 23
Rationale 23
Pre-requisite 24
Unit outcomes 24
2.1 Introduction to Jig Boring 24
2.2 Types of jig boring machine 26
2.3 Methods of locating holes in Jig Boring 27
2.4 Applications of Jig Boring Machine 28
2.5 Moulding 28
2.6 Plastics 29
2.6.1 Types of plastics 30
2.7 Forming and shaping of plastics 30
2.8 Processing of plastics 31
2.8.1 Moulding technique 31
2.8.2 Injection Moulding 32
2.8.3 Compression Moulding 33
2.8.4 Transfer Moulding 35
2.9 Extrusion 36
2.10 Casting 37
2.11 Calendering 37
2.12 Blow Moulding 38
2.13 Lamination and reinforcement 39
2.13.1 Laminated tubes and rods 40
2.14 Plastics 41
2.15 Applications of plastics 41

Know More 42
Summary 42
Exercise 42
References 43

Unit 3: Modern Machining Processes **44-74**
Unit specifics 44
Rationale 44
Pre-requisites 45
Unit outcomes 45
3.1 Introduction 45
3.2 Ultrasonic Machining (USM) 47
3.2.1 Construction of USM 47
3.2.2 Working of Ultrasonic Machining 48
3.2.3 Advantages of Ultrasonic Machining 49
3.2.4 Disadvantages 49
3.2.5 Applications of Ultrasonic Machining 49
3.3 Electrical Discharge Machining (EDM) 49
3.3.1 Principle of EDM 50
3.3.2 Salient Features of EDM 52
3.4 Description of EDM Equipment 53
3.4.1 Tool and Workpiece Electrodes 53
3.4.2 Dielectric Fluid Flushing Unit 54
3.4.3 Pulse Generation Unit 54
3.4.4 Tool Feed Control Unit 56
3.5 EDM Process Parameters 56
3.5.1 Open Circuit, Breakdown and Gap Voltage 56
3.5.2 Peak Current 56
3.5.3 Pulse on Time or Pulse Duration 56
3.5.4 Pulse off Time or Pulse Interval 57
3.5.5 Duty Cycle or Duty Factor 57
3.5.6 Pulse Frequency 57
3.6 Output Characteristics OF EDM 57
3.6.1 Material removal rate (MRR) 57
3.6.2 Tool wear rate (TWR) 57

3.6.3 Overcut (OC) 58
3.6.4 Taper cut 58
3.6.5 Surface roughness 58
3.7 Applications of EDM 59
3.8 Wire Electrical Discharge Machining (Wire EDM) 59
3.8.1 Principle of Wire EDM 60
3.8.2 Crucial Components of Wire EDM 61
3.9 Control Parameters of Wire EDM 61
3.9.1 Pulse-ON time or Spark time 62
3.9.2 Pulse-OFF time or spark pause time 62
3.9.3 Servo or gap voltage 62
3.9.4 Wire feed rate 62
3.9.5 Servo feed 62
3.9.6 Peak current 62
3.9.7 Wire distance between guides 62
3.9.8 Corner dwell time (C-dwell time) 63
3.9.9 Cutting speed over-ride 63
3.9.10 Wire offset 63
3.10 Applications of Wire EDM 63
3.11 Abrasive Water-Jet Machining (AWJM) 63
3.11.1 Working Principle 64
3.12 Laser Beam Machining 69
3.12.1 Principle 69
3.12.2 Working 70
3.13 Electrochemical Machining 71
3.13.1 Principle 71
3.13.2 Construction of ECM 71
3.13.3 Application of ECM 72
Know More 72
Summary 73
Exercise 73
References 74

Unit 4: Machining Center **75-103**
Unit specifics 75

Rationale		75
Pre-requisites		76
Unit outcomes		76
4.1	Introduction	76
4.2	Classification of machining centers	78
	4.2.1 Vertical spindle machining center	78
	4.2.2 Horizontal Machining Center	79
4.3	Automatic tool changer and magazine	79
4.4	Tool magazine	79
4.5	Control System Machine Tool System	80
	4.5.1 Point- to- point system	80
	4.5.2 Straight cut system	80
	4.5.3 Contouring path control system	81
4.6	According to programming methods	81
	4.6.1 Absolute Programming Systems	81
	4.6.2 Incremental Programming systems	82
4.7	According to type of controller	82
	4.7.1 NC based controller systems	82
	4.7.2 CNC based controller system	83
4.8	Common preparatory function (G- codes)	83
4.9	Common Miscellaneous Function (M- codes)	86
4.10	Subroutine	87
4.11	Canned Cycle	87
4.12	Principles of computer-aided part programming	88
4.13	Machine tool automation	89
	4.13.1 Introduction and need	89
4.14	Single spindle automates	90
4.15	Transfer lines	91
4.16	Elements of control system	93
4.17	Limit switches	94
4.18	Proximity switches	96
4.19	Servo Control System	98
4.20	Programmable Logic Controller (PLC)	99
	4.20.1 Introduction to PLCs	99
4.21	Block Diagram of PLC	100

Know More 102
Summary 102
Exercise 102
References 103

Unit 5: Special Purpose Machines (SPMs) **104-119**
Unit specifics 104
Rationale 104
Pre-requisites 105
Unit outcomes 105
5.1 Introduction 105
5.2 General Element of SPM 106
5.3 Productivity Improvement by SPM 107
5.4 Principles of SPM 107
5.5 Maintenance of Machine Tools 109
5.5.1 Preventive maintenance 109
5.5.2 Condition bases maintenance 109
5.5.3 Predictive maintenance 110
5.5.4 Reactive maintenance 110
5.6 Repair cycle analysis 110
5.7 Repair complexity 112
5.8 Maintenance manual 113
5.9 Maintenance records 114
5.10 Housekeeping 115
5.11 Total productive maintenance 117
Know More 118
Summary 119
Exercise 119
References 119

Bibliography **120**
Appendices **122**
CO and PO attainment Table **123**
Index **124**

UNIT 1

JIGS AND FIXTURES

UNIT SPECIFICS

- This unit elaborately discusses the following topics:
- Introduction of Jigs and fixtures
- Types of jigs and general consideration of the design of Jigs
- Types of fixtures
- Basic principles of location, method, and devices
- Basic principles of clamping and types of clamping

Jigs and fixtures are essential tools in manufacturing processes that enhance efficiency, accuracy, and repeatability in machining operations. A jig is a device that guides the cutting tool, ensuring precise positioning and movement, whereas a fixture securely holds the workpiece in place during machining, welding, or assembly. The primary objective of using jigs and fixtures is to achieve consistent quality, reduce human error, and improve productivity by minimizing setup time. Jigs are typically used in drilling, reaming, tapping, and other operations requiring guided tool movement, while fixtures are commonly employed in milling, turning, grinding, and welding processes where stability is critical. Key elements of jigs and fixtures include clamps, locators, supports, and tool-guiding components, each contributing to the overall functionality and reliability of the device. The design of these tools depends on factors such as workpiece shape, production volume, and machining requirements. Standard jigs include template jigs, plate jigs, and box jigs, while common fixtures include milling fixtures, turning fixtures, and modular fixtures. The advantages of using jigs and fixtures include enhanced accuracy, increased safety, reduced manufacturing costs, and improved operational efficiency. They are widely used in industries such as automotive, aerospace, and metalworking, where precision and mass production are crucial.

RATIONALE

The inclusion of a chapter on jigs and fixtures in manufacturing and production studies is essential due to their critical role in improving efficiency, precision, and repeatability in machining operations. In modern manufacturing, where mass production, automation, and quality control are key priorities, understanding jigs and fixtures is fundamental for engineers and technicians. These specialized tools significantly reduce human errors, enhance productivity, and ensure consistent quality by minimizing variations in machining processes.

By studying this chapter, students and professionals will gain insights into the selection, classification, and advantages of jigs and fixtures, along with practical applications in various industries like automotive, aerospace, and tool manufacturing. The knowledge imparted through this chapter fosters innovation in tool design, enabling engineers to create customized solutions for complex machining challenges. Thus, this chapter serves as a foundation for understanding industrial tooling systems and their role in modern production environments.

PRE-REQUISITES

Basics of work holding devices and production engineering

UNIT OUTCOMES

The list of outcomes of this unit is as follows:

U1-O1: Explain various types of jigs and fixtures.

U1-O2: Discuss general considerations in the design of jigs and fixtures.

U1-O3: Explain the principle of location and types of locating devices

U1-O4: Explain the principles of clamping and the types of clamping.

Unit-1 Outcomes	**Expected Mapping with Course Outcomes** *(1- Weak Correlation; 2- Medium correlation; 3- Strong Correlation)*					
	CO-1	**CO-2**	**CO-3**	**CO-4**	**CO-5**	**CO-6**
U1-O1	3	1	2	1	1	2
U1-O2	2	2	1	2	1	1
U1-O3	3	1	2	1	1	2
U1-O4	3	1	2	1	1	2

Introduction

Jigs and fixtures are essential tools in manufacturing that ensure precise replication of parts with increasing the production rate and reduce the human efforts required for production. Ensuring an accurate relationship and position between the cutter, other tools, and the workpiece is of the utmost importance. In order to accomplish this, a jig or fixture is designed to securely hold and position each part, ensuring that every drilling or machining operation is performed within the specified limit.

1.1 Jig

Drilling jigs are meant for mass production setup for operations like drilling, reaming, tapping, counterboring etc. The jigs are normally meant for components having single hole or multiple holes with same/different dimensions. A jig contains minimum four basic elements: (a) body (b) locating system (c) clamping and (d) guide bush.

1.2 Types of Jig

Jigs are utilised to meet the precise processing requirements of the individual components. However, the jigs can be categorised into two types (1) open jig (2) closed jig. Open jigs are used for performing operations exclusively on one side of the component. Closed jigs are utilised for machining component that require processing on many sides.

1.2.1 Leaf Jig

This particular jig has a swinging jig plate that is positioned above the components and has the ability to swing in a vertical direction (**Fig.** 1.1). This type of jigs are small box jigs with hinged leaf to allow for easier loading and unloading. The clamping is provided in the leaf plate. The processing axis is parallel to the loading direction. However, the locating side and processing side at the components are opposite to each other.

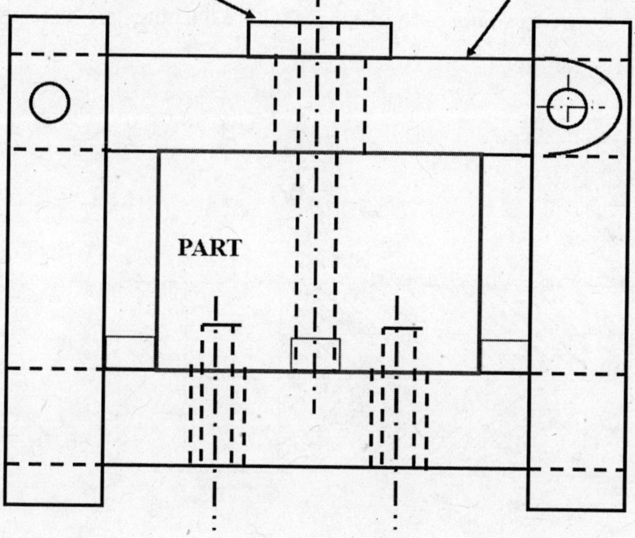

Fig. 1.1 Leaf jig

1.2.2 Box jig

This jig looks like a box, with the locating system situated on one of its vertical plates. Loading or unloading the workpiece occurs in the horizontal direction, while the axis of the hole to be drilled is perpendicular to the loading direction (**Fig.** 1.2). This particular jig design enables the complete machining of the part on all surfaces without the necessity of repositioning the work within the jig.

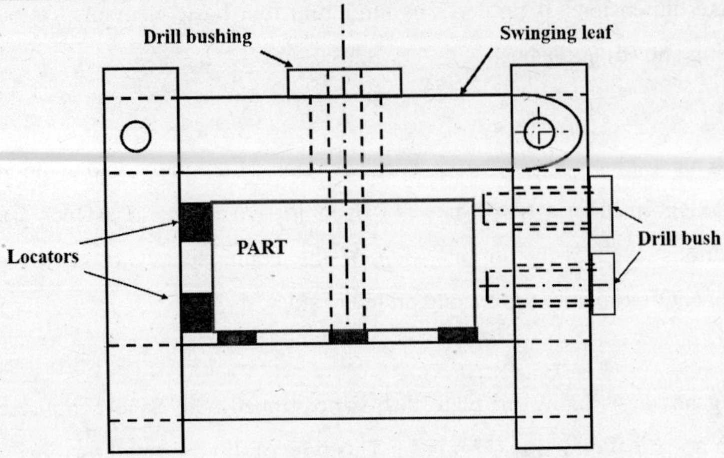

Fig. 1.2 Box jig

1.2.3 Template jig

Template jigs prioritize accuracy over speed in their usage. These jigs are designed to fit over, on, or into the workpiece without requiring clamping (**Fig.** 1.3). They are expensive and simplest to use. This type of jig may or may not use bush. In instances where bushings are absent, the entire jig plate is typically hardened for durability.

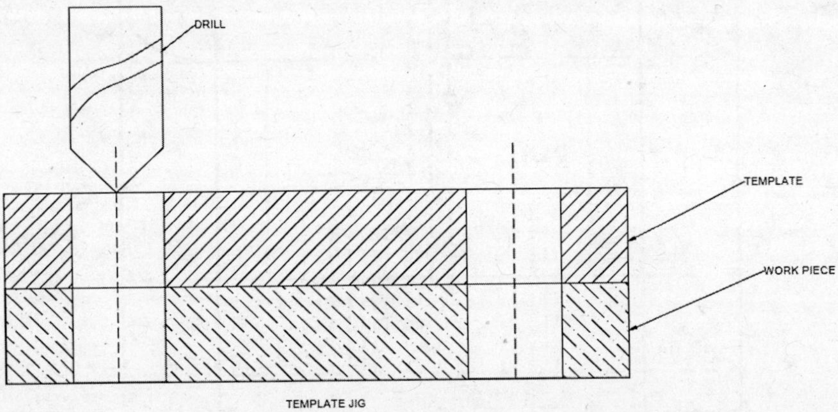

Fig. 1.3 Template jig

1.2.4 Plate Jig

They are similar to templates (**Fig.** 1.4). Plate jigs are distinguished by their integrated clamps, which secure the workpiece in place. They may include bushings or not, depending on the production volume required. Some plate jigs are designed with legs to elevate them above the table, making them suitable for handling larger workpieces. This particular design is referred to as a table jig.

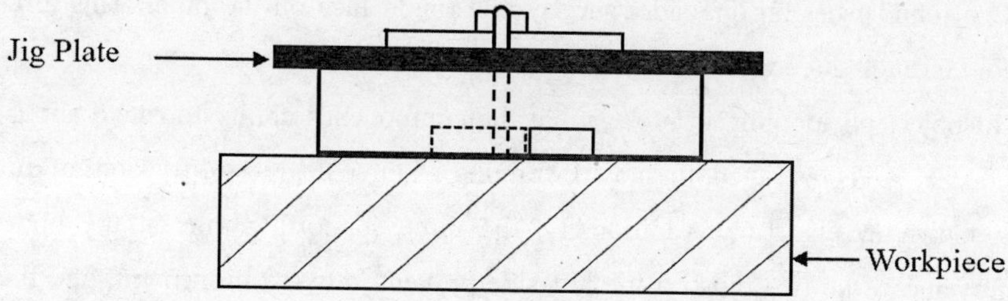

Fig. 1.4. Plate jig

1.2.5 Indexing Jig

Indexing jigs serve the purpose of precisely positioning holes or other machined features around a part with symmetrical peripheral placement and a common point of intersection, as shown in **Fig.** 1.5. This is achieved by utilizing either the part itself or a reference plate along with a plunger. When these jigs are of a larger scale, they are commonly referred to as rotary jigs.

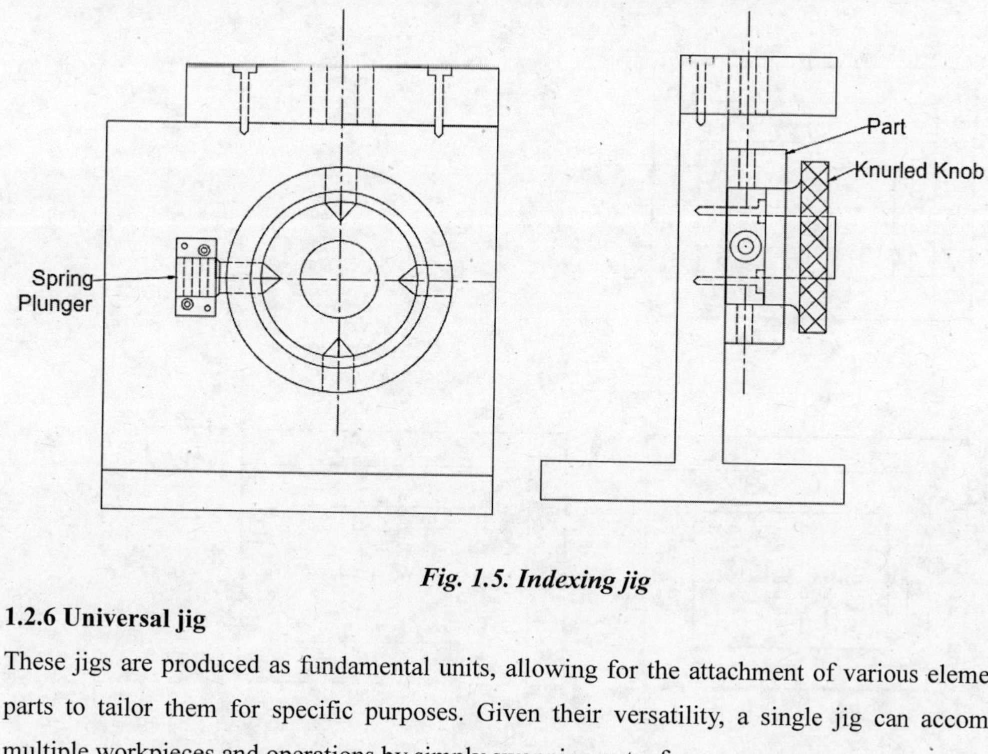

Fig. 1.5. Indexing jig

1.2.6 Universal jig

These jigs are produced as fundamental units, allowing for the attachment of various elements and parts to tailor them for specific purposes. Given their versatility, a single jig can accommodate multiple workpieces and operations by simply swapping out a few components.

1.3 Basic principle of location

According to the described principle, complete restraint of a workpiece can be achieved by providing three location points in one plane, two in a second plane, and one in a third plane. This configuration is illustrated in Fig. 6. In Fig. 6(a), a cube is depicted as being supported at three round faces at the bottom, by two round faces on one side, and by one round face on the other. This arrangement is further clarified through three views shown in Fig. 1.6.

In this type of object positioning, it is clear that the component's ability to rotate about any of the three axes XX, YY, ZZ is restricted, thereby restraining its three degrees of freedom of movement (4, 5, and 6 as shown in Fig. 1.6). Additionally, the three supporting pins at the bottom prevent downward movement, the two pins on the left side prevent leftward movement, and the pin at the rear side prevents backward movement. With all these potential movements restrained, the only remaining free directions of movement are rightward along the axis ZZ and upward along the YY. If attempts are made to further restrict these remaining directions by providing pins on the front, top, and right side, the jig or fixture body would resemble a closed box, making loading or unloading the workpiece impossible. Therefore, these last three degrees of freedom are restrained using clamping devices. This principle is known as the six-point location principle.

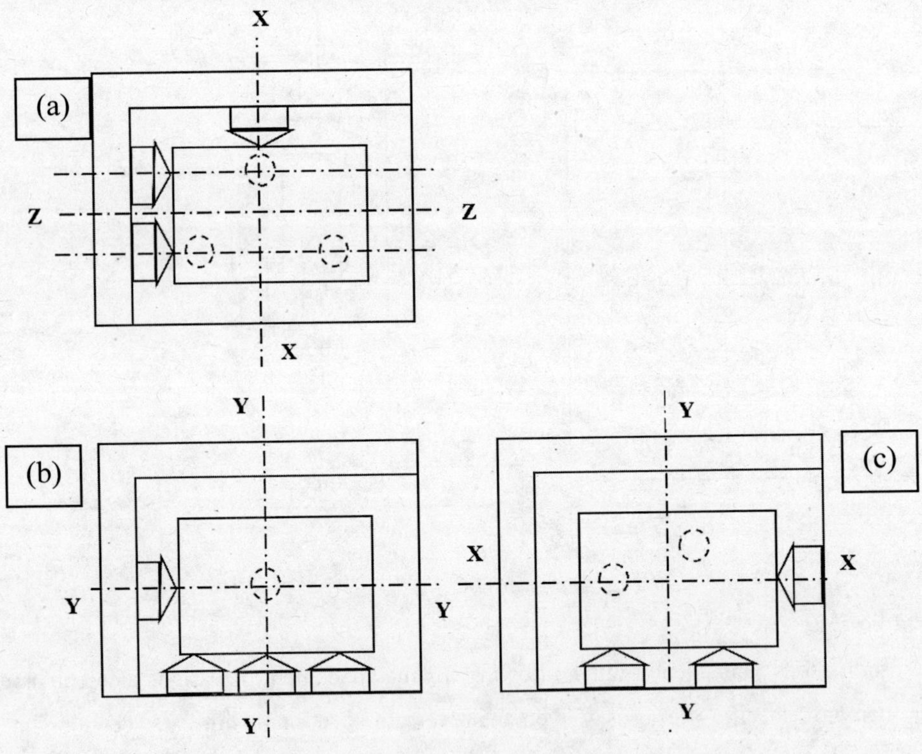

Fig. 1.6. Principle of location (3-2-1 principle)

Locating methods and devices

A jig and fixture designer has a broad range of locating devices and methods available at their end. However, the choice of the most suitable type of locating devices and methods for a particular jig or fixture should be decided carefully, taking into account the following factors:

- Complexity of the shape and size of the workpiece.

- ❖ Type of operation, which the workpiece has to undergo.
- ❖ Number of components to be manufactured.
- ❖ Degree of accuracy desired.
- ❖ Degree of surface finish and accuracy available on the workpiece surface.

Among the most frequently utilized tools for locating the component are pins of varying sizes, V-locators, bush locators, and similar devices. Pins may be of different shapes, such as flat, conical, or cylindrical. Pins are usually made of tempered steel, and are inserted into the body of the jig or fixture through driving or press-fitting. Every pin consists of a locating part and a shank, with a smaller diameter than the locating part. A few typical locators are discussed further:

Pins and buttons: These workpiece locators manage the positioning from either flat surfaces or profiles. A circular pin ensures robust support and proper alignment of the workpiece. The primary distinction between pins and buttons lies in their length, with buttons being shorter and typically utilized for vertical placements. Larger pins may sometimes be referred to as plugs. The accompanying illustration demonstrates a straightforward support pad employed for positioning or supporting the workpiece from a flat surface. The locator fits snugly into the base through an interference fit, while chamfering the locator's bore and undercutting the pad beneath the head ensures a secure seating. If the workpiece requires locating from multiple faces within a given plane, adjustments must be made for the pads and pins on the additional faces. **Fig.** 1.6 (a) showcases a simple adjustable pin or pad. **Figs.** 1.6 (b) and (c) illustrate the use of pins for positioning from a workpiece profile.

Cylindrical locators

Cylindrical post locators are used to position a workpiece through a cylindrical bore feature. Figure 1.7 illustrates a short cylindrical locator that, when combined with a properly qualified base, provides five out of the six locators required in the 3-2-1 location system. When clamping force is applied, this locator restricts all six degrees of freedom except for rotation around its own axis. To achieve complete positioning, additional locators are required to control this rotation. Locators should be precisely aligned with the base and kept as short as possible to avoid binding while loading and unloading the workpiece. If a long locator is used to provide additional support to a weak workpiece, locations must occur only at the ends of the locators.

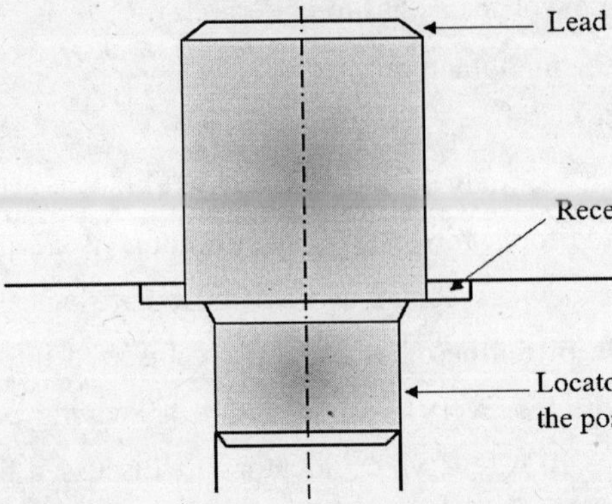

Fig. 1.7. Cylindrical locator

Vee locators: Vee locators provide a very effective, accurate and quick means of locating such workpiece which have circular or semicircular outer surface. The following types of Vee locators are commonly used:

(a) Fixed type vee locators (b) Adjustable type vee locators

Fixed type vee locators: The main locating part of these locators is a V block, with its faces forming vee in vertical plane. But, if these faces are given an inclination of about 3 degrees, the same V-block can be used for locating and clamping both. A fixed type v locators is shown in Fig.1.8. It is fixed to the jig or fixture body by means of Allen screw and dowels as shown in **Fig. 1.8**

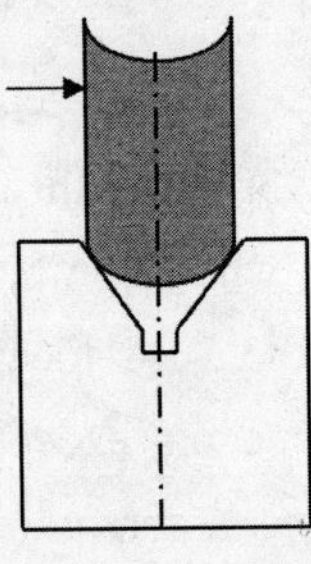

Fig. 1.8. Fixed V- locator

Adjustable type vee locators: Fig. 1.9 shows the adjustable type Vee-locators. The hand nut is provided with a collar, which extends into a slot made in the body of the sliding vee. Consequently, when the hand nut is rotated the sliding vee advances or retards horizontally, together with the axial movement of the screw, depending upon the direction of rotation of the hand nut. The body carries internal threads acts as a nut for the screw. So, when the screw rotates, the nut (body) being fixed, it moves axially inwards to outwards and make the v-locator slide inwards or outwards in the body to locate or/and clamp the workpiece.

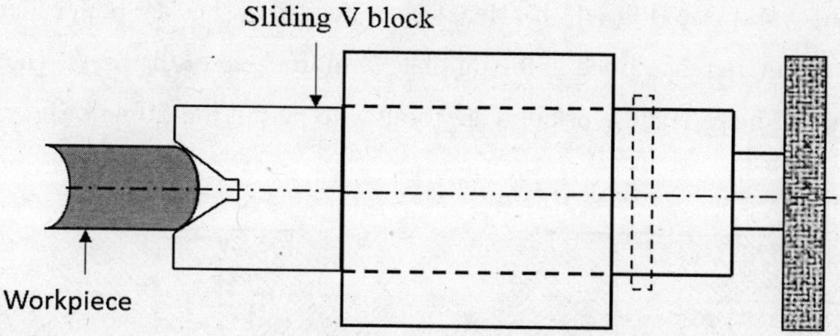

Fig. 1.9. Adjustable V-locators

1.4 Drill Bushes

Bushes are used in jigs to guide drills and reamers to the proper place in the workpiece. They are usually made up of tool steel and fixed in the jig plate or straps. Different bushes are available in the market to suit the needs of the jobs. Some of the bushes are made replaceable so that they can be replaced when worn out.

Types of Drill Bush

- Plain Bush
- Headed bush
- Long bush in two sections

1.4.1 Plain Bush

Headless or plain bushes (Fig. 1.10) are used in cases where the depth of holes is not important. They are the cheapest and are used when a hole is to be produced only by one tool. They are also used when a free surface is required on the top of the jig plate.

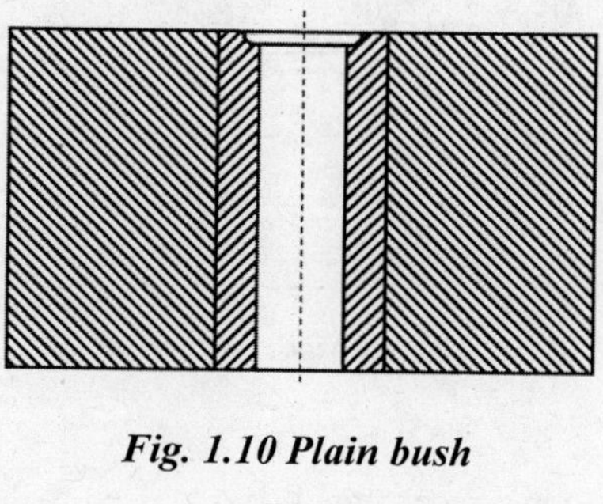

Fig. 1.10 Plain bush

1.4.2 Headed bushes

The headed or flanged bushes are shown in Fig. 1.11(a) and (b). they are used when the hole depth is to be controlled and also when the jig plate into which the bush is to be installed is thin. A good seating of the bush in the seat is ensured by chamfering of the hole and undercutting the head of the bush. A generous lead is provided for the bush and to prevent chips from clogging between the drill plate and the workpiece, the drill bush is either placed close to the workpiece so that the chips can easily escape through the bush (Fig.1.11a) or is placed far enough away to permit chips to escape between it and the workpiece (Fig.1.11 b). Headless or headed bushes are both called fixed or press-fit bushes. There is interference fitted in the jig plate with the help of the press. They are used when the center distance of holes is close or holes are too low to permit the fitting of liners and renewable bushes.

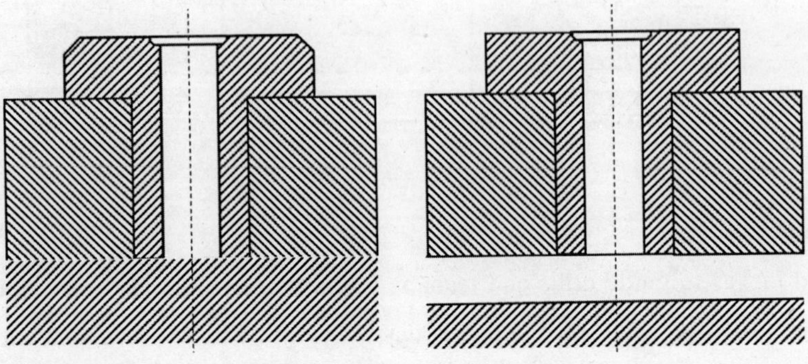

(a) (b)

Fig. 1.11 Headed Bush

1.4.3 Long bush in two sections

A long bush may also be sometimes designed in two sections, as shown Fig. 1.12. The longer bush can be made of a cheaper material like C.I., and only the lower actual drill bush needs to be made of more costly bush material. This considerably reduces the cost of the bush.

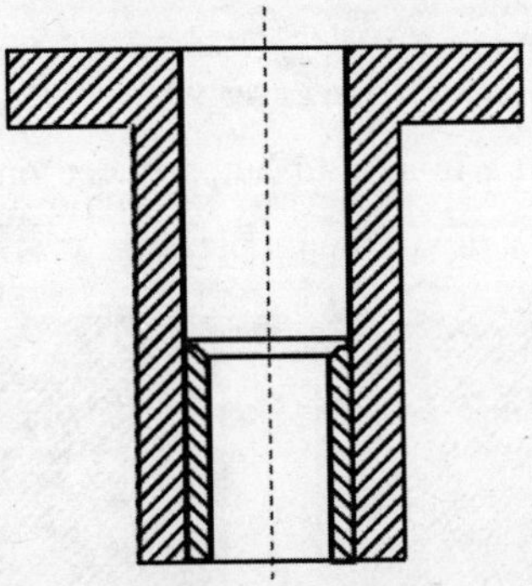

Fig. 1.12 Long bush in two sections

1.5 Vice Fixture

A vise (or vice) fixture (Fig. 1.13) is a mechanical device used to secure an object to allow work to be performed on it. Vises have a variety of applications, including in woodworking, metalworking, and general mechanical work.

Components of a Vice Fixture

Body:

The main structure that supports other components. Typically made of cast iron or steel for strength and durability.

Jaws:

Fixed Jaw: Stationary part of the vise.

Movable Jaw: Adjusts to clamp the workpiece.

Jaws often have replaceable faces to grip different materials.

Screw Mechanism:

Operates the movable jaw. Consists of a threaded screw that turns to move the jaw.

Handle:

Attached to the screw mechanism. Turned by the operator to open or close the jaws.

Base:

The foundation that mounts the vise to a workbench or stand. May be fixed or swivel, allowing for rotation.

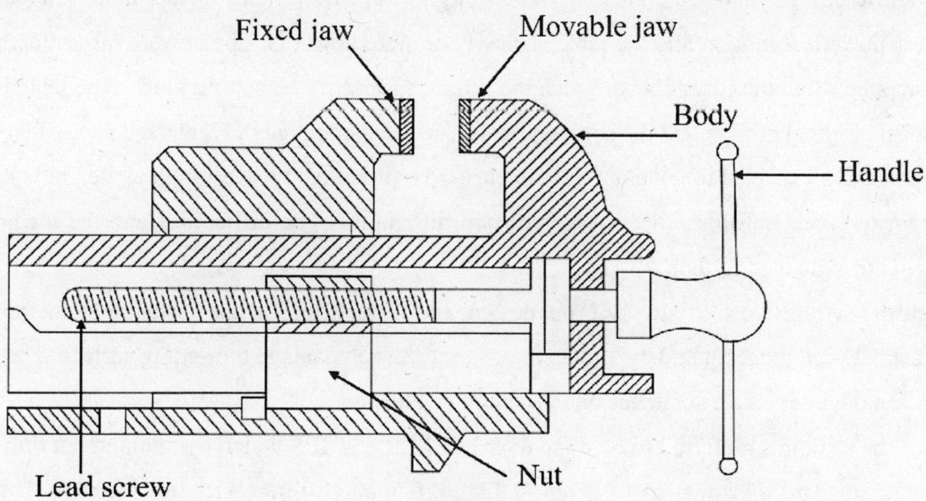

Fig. 1.13. Vice fixture

1.6 Milling Fixtures

Milling fixtures are used on vertical milling machines as well as the horizontal milling machines. The fixtures consist of the elements like a body, some locating system, and clamping system. As at the drilling jigs, the cutter does not remain in guided condition while performing its job on the component. But its position has to be fixed up before commencement of the operation. Subsequently, the only freedom given to the cutter (relative to the workpiece position) is in the feed direction. This task of positioning the cutter with respect to the fixture (in turn with respect to the component) is assigned to an element called as a SETTING BLOCK. The setting block is used to set the cutter at the Y (transversal) and z (vertical) direction. The x (longitudinal, along the length of table) direction is left open for the feed purpose.

The jigs are permitted to be placed at any convenient place on the table of the machine because the drill mounted on the spindle of the radial drilling machine can reach any desired position. But such freedom can not be available by a milling fixture since the milling cutter carries a fixed position. The desires placement of the fixture on the table, especially in the y direction and around the z direction, is achieved by a means of TENONS. Now let us know more about the setting block and the tenon.

Refer **Fig.** 1.14, imagine the setting of the cutter for its vertical setting. For maintaining a height H at the component, the cutting plane has to be at identical height from the rest pads. Hence the cutter face has to be set at level H. Using a setting block this task is effectively performed.

The setting block is a hard metal block secured to the fixture by means of bolting and dowel pins. The setting block carries a highly accurate setting plane exposed to the rotating cutter. While carrying out the setting, initially the fixture with setting block shall be much below the cutter. The setting block shall be brought under the cutter by necessary upward movement of the table. The cutter is given slow powerless motion and the table is slowly brought upwards. The upward movement of the table is stopped when the cutting teeth touch the setting surface of the setting block. The table is now locked for its vertical motion and the setting now is said to be completed. Now the cutter, when fed to the component, is expected to generate the dimension H, provided the setting block height is kept as (H+t) from its base. But this process involves two difficulties. The difficulties and the methods to solve them are explained further.

1) When the setting block is slowly brought near the cutter teeth, at the instance of the physical contact between the teeth and the block, the cutter teeth can damage the setting surface. The cutter teeth can dig in or create scratches which cannot be allowed.

   Hence the setting is preferred to be done over FEELER STRIPS which are nothing but thin metal strips of standard thickness like 0.1mm, 0.25mm, 0.5mm, 1.0 mm, etc. If a feeler of 0.5mm is planned to be used, then the setting block height shall be reduced to (H+ t-0.5) mm. While setting the cutter, the feeler strip is firmly placed over the setting surface and the cutter teeth contact is now established over the feeler strip surface. The feeler strip, when spoiled, can be thrown off.

   Paper feeler is seen to be a convenient feeler. A common paper measures 0.8 mm at its thickness. A small piece of such paper, dipped in oil, is pasted over the setting surface. When the slow rotating cutter touches the paper feeler, the paper strip gets swept away by the cutter and setting gets established. Hence, while recommending the use of paper feeler, the setting block is made to its height equal to (H+t-0.08) mm. Necessary instruction is stamped at the base of setting block which may read as "Use 0.08 mm Paper Feeler".

2) While taking the cut on the component, the cutter may cover the component and setting block simultaneously, if the setting block is placed very near to the component. This is also objectionable because due to jerks and vibrations, the cutter teeth are likely to touch the setting

block in power driven condition. Hence, it is preferred that the space between the workpiece and the setting block has to be larger than the cutter diameter. Such arrangement ensures the cutter to be away from the setting block when doing normal cutting operations.

The cutter mentioned at the **Fig.** 1.14 (a) was meant for a Vertical Milling Machine and was generating only one cutting plane and one machined surface. But the cutters used on Horizontal Milling Machines can generate two vertical surfaces and one horizontal surface at the component. At such cases, it is equally important to set the vertical cutting plane also. The setting block at this case carries two setting surfaces as shown at the **Fig.** 1.14 (b). The setting is done first on the horizontal setting surface, the vertical position of the table is now locked and the setting process is repeated at the vertical setting surface. Subsequently, the Y direction movement is locked.

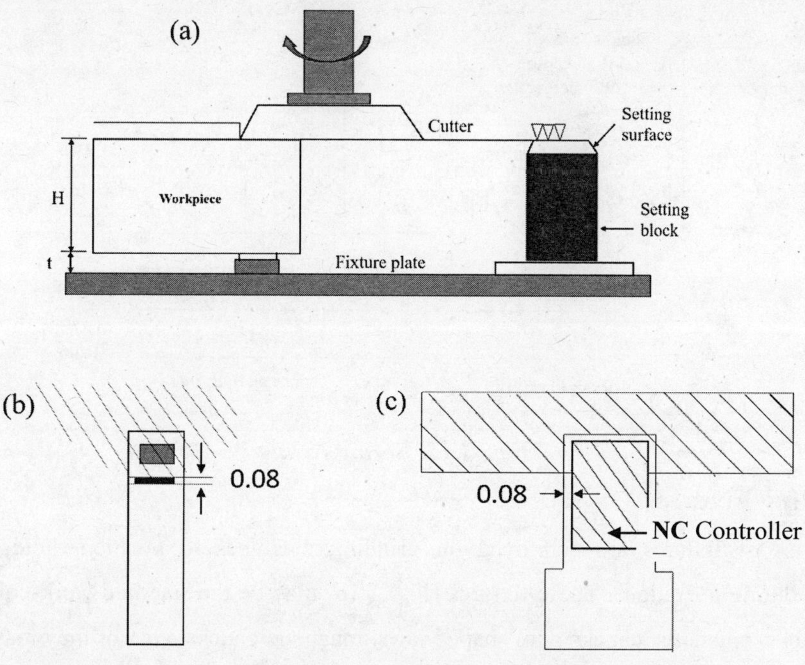

Fig. 1.14. (a) Vertical milling machine (b) Setting block (c) Tenon

As stated earlier, placement of the fixture on the table of the milling machine, at a specific place with respect to the Y direction, is equally important. The Tenons are used for this purpose. The tenons are nothing but a pair of rectangular shaped metal pieces screwed to this fixture plate from the bottom side. A slot is milled throughout or at the end portion of the length of the fixture and the tenons are fitted in the slot towards the ends of the fixture and subsequently screwed there. These tenons are supposed to be located in the central longitudinal T slot of the milling machine table. Refer **Fig.** 1.14 (c).

The tenons and the central T slot are required to have a precise fitment of the order of H8 – e8 or H8 - f8 etc. This fitment disallows the fixture to have any displacement in y direction, and rotation around z axis. Accordingly, the setting done in the y direction using the setting block, gets preserved. The central "T" slot of the milling machine table is thus meant for tenon fitment and the clamping of the fixture is preferred to be done only at the first and the third slot only. Such practice preserves the accuracy of the central slot and subsequently the tenon fitment.

1.7 Boring Fixture

While these fixtures incorporate many common jig and fixture design principles, their construction need not be as robust as milling fixtures, since they do not experience the same level of heavy cutting forces. As shown in Fig. 1.15, the primary purpose of this fixture is to secure the workpiece in the proper position relative to the boring bar. Since they aren't subject to strong cutting forces, boring fixtures don't need to be as sturdy.

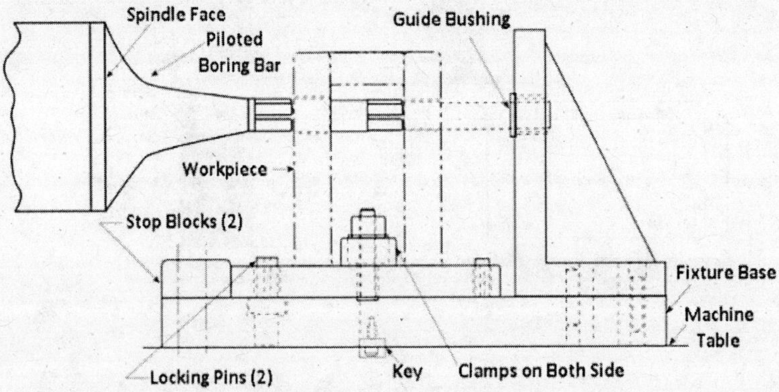

Fig. 1.15. Boring fixture

1.8 Grinding Fixtures

Various types of fixtures are employed on grinding machines to position, hold, and support workpieces during operations. These fixtures (Fig. 1.16) may be the standard work-holding devices, such as chucks, mandrels, chucks with shaped jaws, magnetic chucks, etc., or they may be specially designed to suit the complex shapes of workpieces, type of operation, machine capacity, etc. For example, A vertical surface grinder with a rotary table often includes a rotary fixture mounted on the table. For surface grinders with a reciprocating table, a plain or string fixture may be used. A common example of a standard grinding fixture designed for shaping drill geometry is the drill grinding attachment. When designing fixtures for grinding operations, it is essential to provide for coolant flow and drainage, allow for the attachment of wheel dressers, and maintain balance for rotating fixtures.

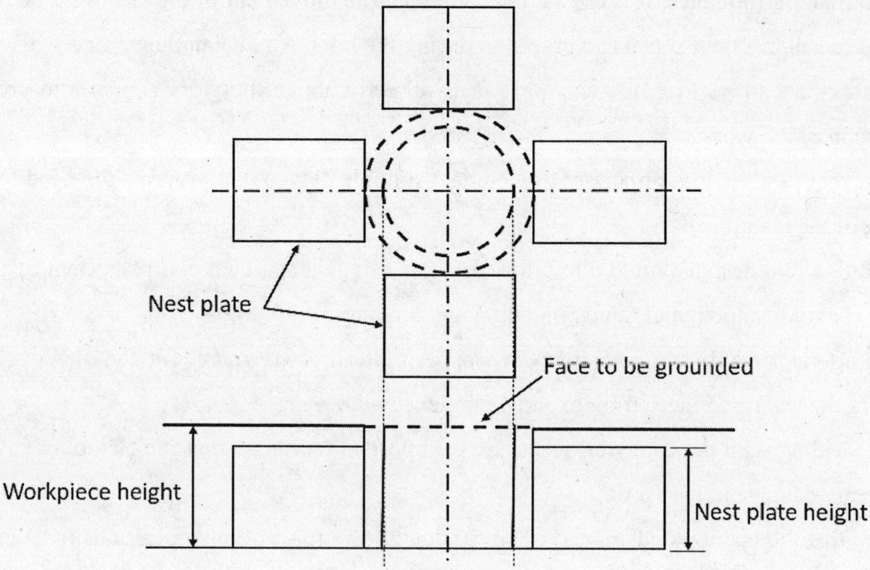

Fig. 1.16. Grinding fixture

1.9 Important considerations in clamp design

When designing clamping devices for jigs and fixtures, it's essential to adhere to fundamental principles to ensure their efficient operation and alignment with operational requirements. Several factors must be considered during the design process to ensure that these devices effectively serve their intended purpose. Following are some key considerations include:

1. It should be easy to use, efficient, and error-free.
2. The device should be capable of applying the necessary clamping pressure to the workpiece with minimal force.
3. Nevertheless, it is important to maintain the clamping pressure at a level that is sufficient to secure the workpiece against any external forces. Excessive clamping pressure can negatively affect the quality of the work.
4. Ensure that the clamping pressure on the workpiece is directed in a way that effectively counters the external forces.
5. It is important to ensure that the clamping pressure is directed in the same direction as the cutting process, whenever possible.
6. It is important to ensure that both the clamping pressure and cutting forces are applied to the locating surface or pins in order to avoid any bending or distortion of the workpiece.
7. Ensure that the clamping pressure is applied towards the support surfaces and/or point in order to prevent any lifting of the workpiece from its support.
8. The clamp needs to have a sturdy construction to ensure it remains strong and doesn't deform when subjected to pressure.

9. For optimal performance, it is crucial to ensure that the movement of the clamp is controlled and guided to achieve both speed and precision during the release and clamping process.
10. It is important to position the clamping faces directly above the work supports to prevent any distortion of the work.
11. Whenever possible, it is important to include a suitable device that prevents the need for manual lifting of the clamp.
12. In addition, the design should allow for easy and efficient removal and placement of the clamp form, ensuring smooth and rapid unloading and loading.
13. It is important to always recommend an appropriate heat treatment for the clamp in order to prevent the clamping faces from experiencing excessive wear.
14. When dealing with delicate workpieces, it is important to ensure that the clamping faces do not cause any damage to the work.
15. Ensure that the clamp is positioned in a way that allows for multiple operations to be carried out on the workpiece without disrupting the clamp's setting.

1.9.1 TYPE OF CLAMPS

1.9.1.1 Strap Clamp

A strap clamp is an assembly of a strap plate with built in heel portion, a stud mounted in the body of the Jig / Fixture, a washer and a nut. Here, the clamping action is generated at the screw center line and subsequently transferred to the component covering a distance "a." The heel portion can be integral with the main strap plate. But at this style, its height is required to be carefully maintained to match the component height. Otherwise, the heel portion can be separate pin with adjustable height. The engagement of the strap with the component can be rotated through 90° around the stud axis. In such case, the strap may have a simple plain hole to accommodate the stud. In the second option, the scrap can contain a slot of appropriate length so that it can be pulled out / pushed in shown in Fig. 1.17. for an illustration of such case. The stud position of the clamp assembly with respect to the component and the heel also plays an important role. The proportion between the distance between a and b determines the share of the clamping effort being passed on to the component. The distance a is preferred to be proportionately small as compared with b. While unloading / loading any component, the strap clamp assembly is not required to be dismantled. The strap clamp is generally not used in single but in pairs on opposite sides of the component.

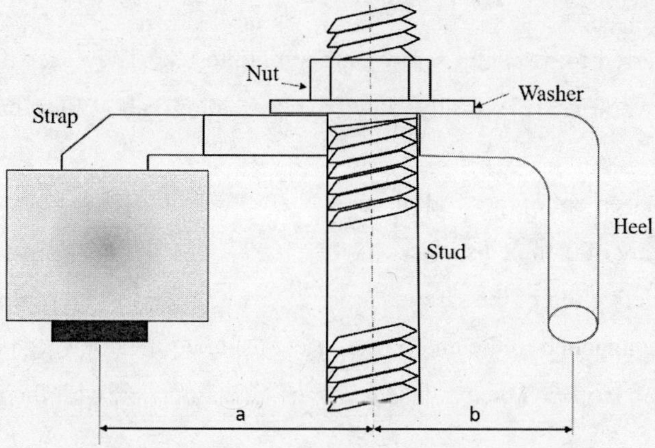

Fig. 1.17. Strap clamp

1.9.1.2 Cam operated clamps

Various designs of cam operated clamps are available, including direct acting lever clamp, shaft eccentric clamps, and more. An example of the direct acting lever clamp is illustrated in **Fig.** 1.18. This design features a strap clamp where the clamping stud does not require a nut. The top of the stud is designed to hold an eye, where the pin is inserted. The camera is attached to this pin and can be moved down to secure or up to release the strap and, therefore, the workpiece. For increased pressures, opting for the shaft eccentric type 'cam operated clamp' mentioned earlier is recommended. It is a type of swing clamp, in which usually a swing both is used. The bolt may be operated by an eccentric or it may be hinged at one end. It is quite effective for light clamping and is fairly quick-acting. It quite useful in confined spaces.

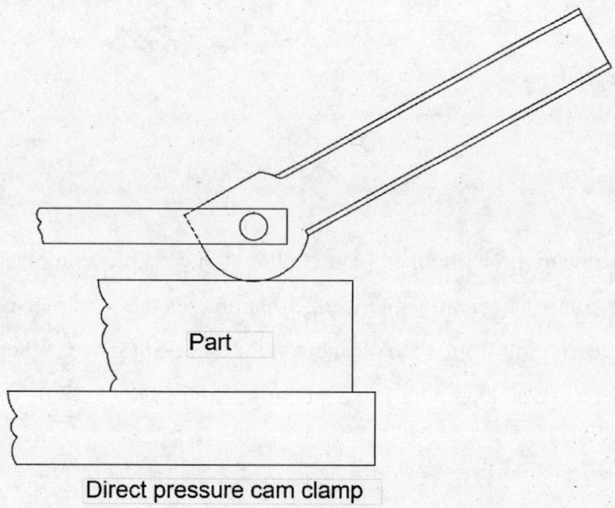

Fig. 1.18. Direct pressure cam operated clamp

1.9.1.3 Screw Clamps:

These clamps, also referred to as clamp screws, are simple to use. They exert force directly on the lateral surfaces of the workpiece. Typically, they have a floating pad at their end for the following reasons:

- To prevent displacement of the workpiece
- To prevent denting of clamped surface
- To prevent the deflection of the screw

The floating pad can be attached to the end of the screw using a pin, screw, or ball. The second type is depicted in **Fig.** 1.19. However, some disadvantages are associated with the use of these clamps, as given below:

- The clamping force is not constant. It varies from workpiece to workpiece.
- Relatively larger effort is needed for clamping resulting in fatigue to the operator.
- In the absence of floating pads, the component may shift due to frictional forces, and the screw tip can leave indentation marks on the clamped surface.
- The time taken in more, particularly if a number of such clamps are employed for clamping the workpiece from clamping the workpiece from different sides.

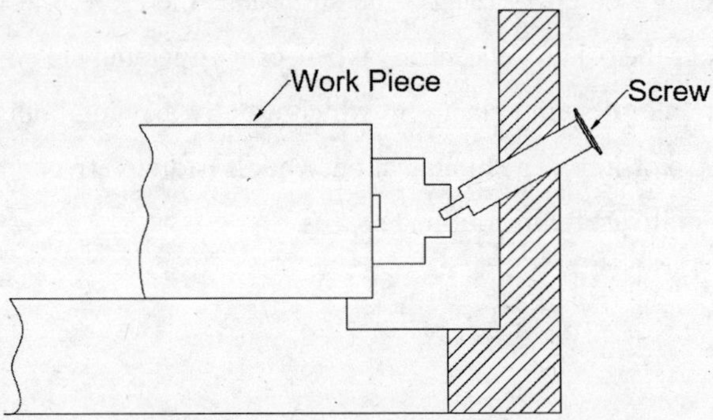

Fig. 1.19. Screw clamp

1.9.1.4 Wedge clamps

These clamps use the concept of an inclined plane to hold the workpiece in place. Illustrated in Fig. 1.20 is a wedge clamp comprising a movable wedge that presses the workpiece against a fixed stop. The wedge has an angle ranging from 1° to 4° and can hold itself in place. When the wedge moves horizontally, it creates a vertical clamping force on the workpiece.

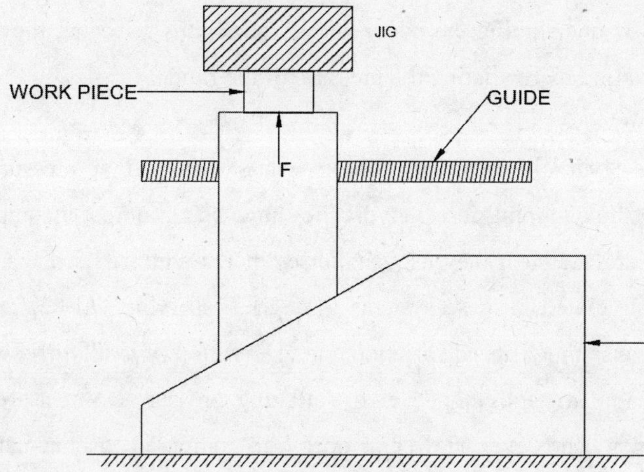

Fig. 1.20. Wedge clamp

1.9.1.5 Toggle clamps

Toggle clamp as shown in Fig. 1.21 carry a number of sturdy and rigid links, which are moved in a definite manner to affect the required clamping. They are so designed that the movement of small movement of a fork. But, for releasing the clamp there has to be a larger movement in a direction normal to the direction of clamping force. A toggle clamp may affect the clamping of a workpiece through one of the following actions:

- By holding down the workpiece
- By pulling the workpiece against a fixed surface
- By sliding (a liner motion)
- By compressing the workpiece between two surfaces.

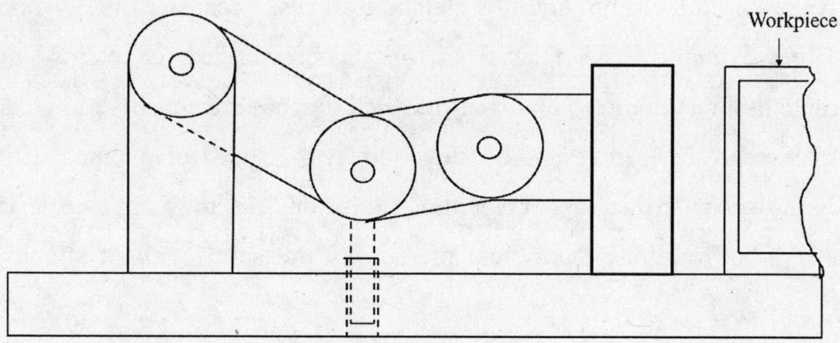

Fig. 1.21. Toggle clamp

1.9.1.6 Pneumatic and hydraulic clamps:

Hydraulic and pneumatic clamps are grouped under fluid power clamping devices because both these types of clamps use the pressure of a fluid to apply the clamping force. The schematic diagram for a typical fluid power clamping system is shown in Fig. 1.22 and Fig. 1.23. Oil and Air pressure in the cylinder is used for providing the clamping force. The force of the fluid is transmitted to the clamp through the link shown. For unclamping the piston moves back thus releasing the workpiece. The clamping pressure can be varied by regulating the pressure of the fluid.

❖ **Hydraulic clamping:**

The Fig. 1.19 shows the Hydraulic clamping system which uses oil at pressure of 7 to 250 atmospheres for providing the clamping force. Hydraulic fluids being almost incompressible can be used to exert higher pressure. As such they use smaller cylinders and are used for exerting higher clamping force. Oil is recirculated in these systems through a reservoir. Oil being incompressible hydraulic systems do not cause much speed variation due to variation of load. Speed variation can be further minimized to an almost negligible level by utilizing pressure-compensated flow control valves. Hydraulic systems are, however, slower in operation compared to pneumatic systems and require substantially higher initial investment.

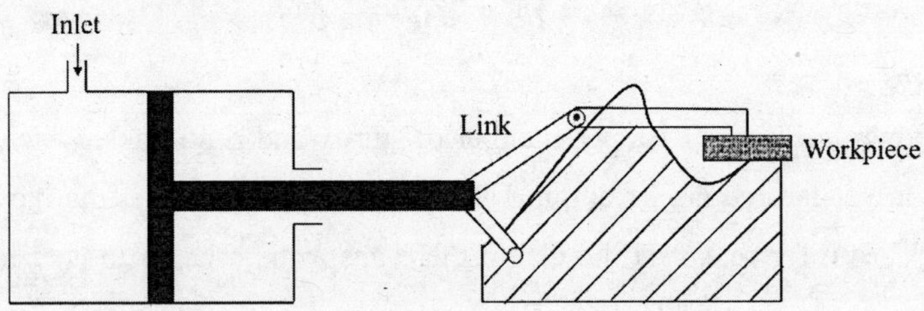

Fig. 1.22. Hydraulic Clamp

❖ **Pneumatic clamping:**

Pneumatic clamping, shown in Fig. 1.23, employs compressed air as the fluid for providing clamping force. The pressure of the air used is from 5 to 6 atmospheres. Generally, a large centralized compressor supplies pressurized air to all the pneumatic drives and fixtures in the shop. Pneumatic clamping devices are used for supplying low clamping forces. Because of the lower pressures these devices need larger cylinders. The exhaust air, once depressurized, is released directly into the atmosphere through a direct control valve. Air-operated devices are sensitive to changes in the load they handle. An increase in load resistance slows down the speed of pneumatic devices, while a decrease causes the speed to increase. Over time, these devices may develop leaks at the joints, leading to energy loss. To adjust the system pressure, a pressure regulator should be installed in the line.

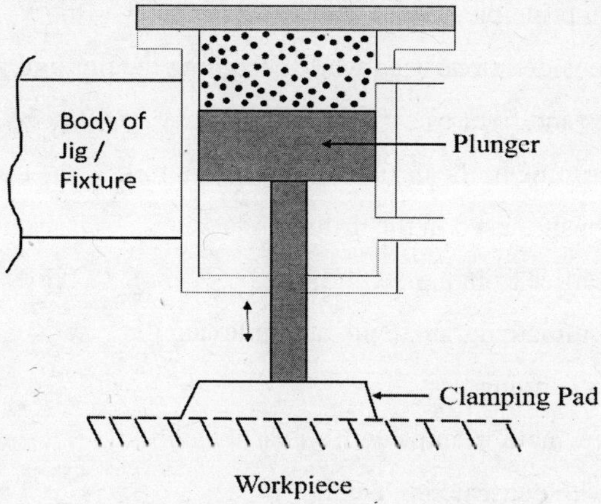

Fig. 1. 23: Pneumatic clamp

KNOW MORE

More about jig and fixtures

SUMMARY

Jigs and fixtures are essential in manufacturing to guide tools and secure workpieces, ensuring accuracy and efficiency. Jigs guide cutting tools and include types like leaf jigs, box and handle jigs, template jigs, plate jigs, indexing jigs, universal jigs, and vice jigs. They emphasize alignment, stability, and ease of handling. Fixtures used to hold workpieces include vice fixtures, milling fixtures, boring fixtures, and grinding fixtures, designed for specific operations with locator pins and clamps for precision. The design of jigs and fixtures follows principles of location and clamping. The location ensures correct alignment using surfaces, pins, or slots to restrict movement, while clamping secures the workpiece without deformation. Common clamps include strap, cam, screw, toggle, and hydraulic or pneumatic clamps for efficiency and automation. These tools enhance machining accuracy and productivity.

EXERCISE

1. What are the advantages of employing jigs and fixtures in mass-production work?
2. Write and briefly discuss the basic elements of Jigs and Fixture.

3. Explain the 3-2-1 location principle.
4. List the general design considerations used while designing the jigs and fixtures.
5. Differentiate between Jigs and fixtures
6. What is meant by fool proofing in the design of jigs and fixtures?
7. Briefly comment on the bushes used in the drilling jigs.
8. How does a template jig differ from a plate jig?
9. Give neat sketches of a template jig, plate jig, and indexing jig.
10. Write basic principles of clamping
11. Explain hydraulic and pneumatic clamps with a neat sketch.
12. Explain boring fixtures with construction detail.

REFERENCES

1. Manufacturing Process II, "Jigs and fixtures for machine shop" Module 8 NPTEL, https://archive.nptel.ac.in/courses/112/105/112105127/#
2 https://sripc.edu.in/data/uploads/td/Notes/5%20Sem/4022510%20JFG%20_%20V%20sem%20TD%20Notes%20Of%20Lesson.pdf

UNIT 2 JIG BORING AND PLASTIC PROCESSING

UNIT SPECIFICS

The following points are discussed in the following section:

- Introduction of jig boring and types of jig boring
- System of the location of holes
- Introduction to plastic processing and types of plastic processing
- Exploring the various types of fabrication methods for sheet forming, blow molding, tubes, and rods

Jig boring and plastic processing are two distinct yet essential manufacturing techniques used in precision engineering and material shaping. Jig boring is a highly accurate machining process used for creating precise holes, locating features, and finishing surfaces with tight tolerances. Unlike conventional drilling, jig boring uses specialized boring machines equipped with precision control systems to achieve extreme accuracy in hole placement and size. This technique is commonly applied in industries such as aerospace, automotive, and die manufacturing, where precision is crucial. The key components of jig boring machines include high-speed spindles, fine feed mechanisms, and rigid structures to ensure minimal vibrations and maximum accuracy.

On the other hand, plastic processing involves various techniques for shaping and molding plastic materials into desired products. It encompasses methods such as injection molding, compression, transfer, extrusion, and blow molding, each suited for different applications. Injection molding is widely used for mass production of plastic components, while extrusion is ideal for creating continuous profiles like pipes and sheets. Plastic processing plays a significant role in industries such as packaging, consumer goods, medical devices, and automotive manufacturing due to its cost-effectiveness, lightweight nature, and design flexibility.

RATIONALE

The establishment of a jog boring and plastic processing unit is a strategic initiative driven by the growing demand for precision machining and plastic-based components across various industries. Jig boring, a specialized machining process, is essential for manufacturing high-precision parts required in automotive, aerospace, heavy machinery, and industrial manufacturing sectors. Additionally, the plastic processing industry has witnessed significant growth due to its widespread application in packaging, construction, automotive, electronics, and healthcare. The increasing demand for sustainable and recyclable plastic materials further strengthens the business case for a plastic processing unit. Advanced plastic processing techniques such as injection molding, extrusion, and blow molding enable high-volume and high-quality production of plastic components.

PRE-REQUISITE

Basics of Jig and Fixtures and Basic Manufacturing Processes

UNIT OUTCOMES

The list of outcomes of this unit is as follows:

U2-O1: Explain the construction and working of different types of jig boring machines.

U2-O2: Describe the systems of locating holes.

U2-O3: Explain the types of the molding process.

U2-O4: Explain the different types of fabrication methods for sheet forming, rods, and tubes, and applications of plastic processing.

Unit-2 Outcomes	Expected Mapping with Course Outcomes (*1- Weak Correlation; 2- Medium correlation; 3- Strong Correlation*)					
	CO-1	**CO-2**	**CO-3**	**CO-4**	**CO-5**	**CO-6**
U2-O1	3	3	2	1	1	3
U2-O2	3	3	2	1	1	2
U2-O3	3	3	2	3	1	3
U2-O4	3	3	3	3	1	3

2.1 Introduction to Jig Boring

Jig boring is a high-precision machining process used to position and size holes accurately, employing specialized machines like open-front and cross-rail types with rigid construction and precise alignment systems. Additionally, plastic processing involves moulding techniques such as injection, compression, and transfer moulding, as well as extrusion, casting, and calendering for creating various forms. Fabrication methods like sheet forming, blow moulding, laminating, and reinforcing enhance the versatility of plastics, making them integral to industries like packaging, construction, and automotive.

Working principle

The feed is provided relative to the vertical axis of the hole and its radius. In this method, the rotating tool moves over the stationary workpiece to perform the operation. This principle is used for large work pieces. For small size workpieces, the tool is kept stationary, and work is moved by applying force. The jig boring is a special type of boring process; hence its working principle is just similar to the boring process.

Construction

The jig boring machine is shown in Fig. 2.1. The table provides a longitudinal motion to the workpiece.

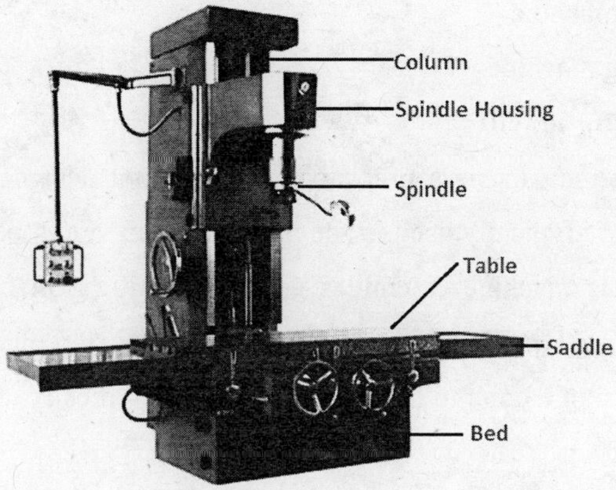

Fig.2.1. Photo of jig Boring machine

The table is arranged on saddle. It can move in different on the guide ways of the saddle. A spindle head is provided at the top of this column, which is fixed on the guideways of the column. The spindle is fixed using a preloaded antifriction bearing. Jig boring machine generally consists of a heavy base and a column, and by moving the spindle head up and down,. the vertical movement of the spindle is obtained. Saddle cross movement to the workpiece. The main components of the jig boring machine are as follows.

Head-stock

The headstock is also called the spindle head. It is fixed on a column on the front side. The spindle moves inside the quill and is supported by the housing or spindle head. The movement of this quill in an up-and-down motion increasingly appears like a mechanism suitable for telescoping applications.

Column

A hollow component made from cast iron (C.I.). It supports the headstock and guideways, and the vertical head provides an axis for positioning.

Bed

The part of the machine that serves as its foundation is called the bed. Made of cast iron, it supports the column, saddle, control panel, and the entire machine.

Pick up devices

It is connected to both the table and saddle and assists in automatically controlling various machine operations. Additionally, devices are required for precise measurement.

Table and saddle

The table is designed to secure and hold the workpiece in a fixture at the desired position, which is why it features T-shaped slots. The saddle allows for the longitudinal movement of the workpiece.

2.2 Types of jig boring machine

There are mainly two types of jig boring machine

I. Single column jig boring machine

II. Double column jig boring machine

I. Single column jig boring machine

A single-column jig boring machine is a precision machine tool designed for drilling and boring holes with high accuracy. It is typically used in the manufacturing and tool-making industries where precision is paramount. This machine resembles a vertical milling machine, which is why it is referred to as a vertical milling-type jig boring machine. It consists of a plain rotary table, an inclined table, and a square table. A single-column jig boring machine is typically used for machining smaller components.

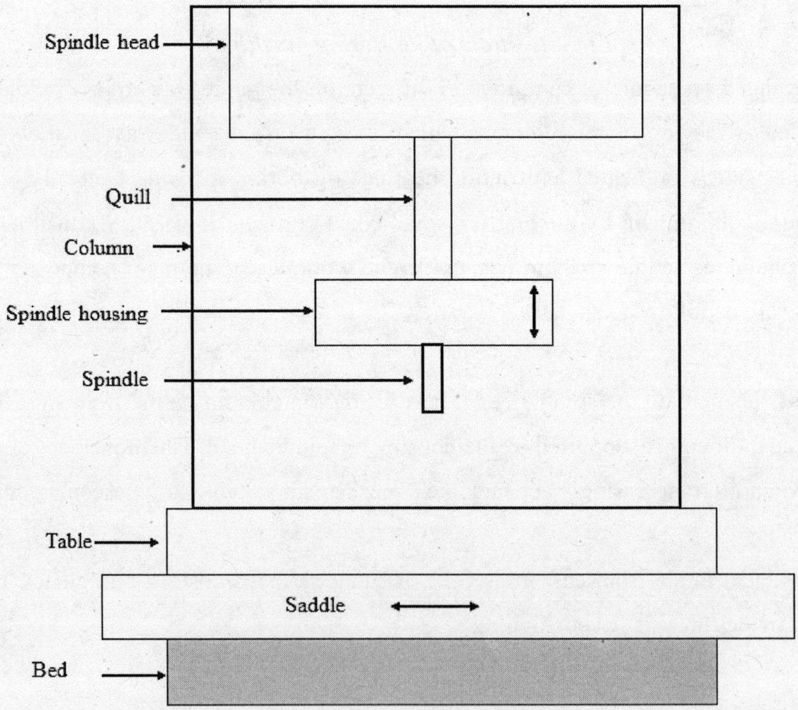

Fig. 2.2. Single column jig boring machine

II. Double-column jig boring machine

The double-column jig boring machine is shown in Figure 2.3. This machine is also called a planer-type machine. The machine features two vertical columns positioned on either side of the table and securely mounted to the base. The table moves back and forth to allow for workpiece adjustments, while the spindle is mounted on the crossrail connecting the two vertical columns.

In a planer-type jig borer, hole positioning is achieved through two coordinated movements: the table's longitudinal motion and the spindle's crosswise movement along the Cross-rail.

Working

The following section details the explanation of the working of a single-column or double column jig boring machine. Ensure the workpiece is properly cleaned or free from any debris. If it is necessary mark the location for drilling or boring and select the appropriate tool. Properly align the workpiece on the table using the dial indicator. Then, set initial coordinates for the X and Y axes using the machine control panel. After setting all the coordinates, move the spindle to the starting position above the first location, then lower the spindle using the set parameter until the cutting tool contacts the workpiece. Engage the spindle to start the drilling or boring operation. If multiple holes are required, reposition the workpiece or move the worktable to the next location. Repeat the drilling or boring process for each hole.

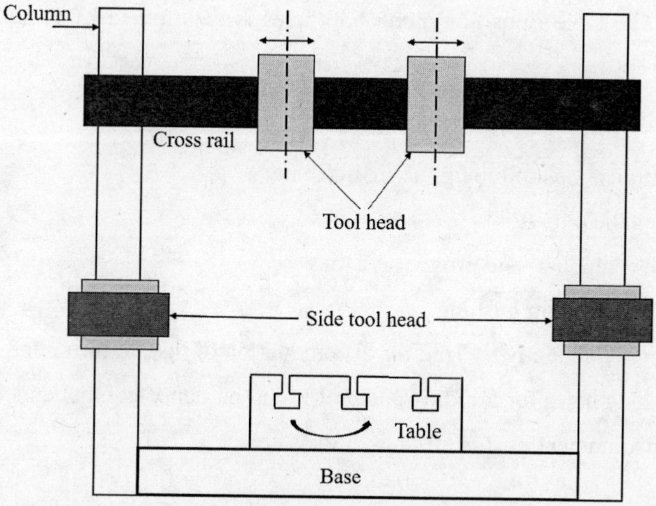

Fig. 2.3 Double-column jig boring

2.3 Methods of locating holes in Jig Boring

Holes on jigs and fixtures should be drilled at specific distances from the two straight edges of the workpiece. Precise placement is crucial for creating accurate jigs, fixtures, dies, and similar tools.

The primary operation in a jig boring machine is achieving precise hole positioning. Accurate hole location in a jig boring machine can be accomplished using any of the following methods:

- Leadscrew method
- Mechanical and electrical gauging method
- Optical measuring method.

Leadscrew Method

The leadscrew method represents the predominant and most efficient technique for positioning the workpiece beneath the spindle. The longitudinal and cross-feed lead screws are adjusted to predetermined values. Errors in the lead screw resulting from backlash, wear, or manufacturing defects can be rectified through the use of a compensating device.

Mechanical and Electrical Gauging Method

Mechanical gauges, like gauge blocks or end measures, are positioned against a stop on the table, with a dial indicator attached to the outer end of the setup. The table's movement is guided by the length of the end measures, allowing precise positioning in both longitudinal and crosswise directions to locate the hole accurately. Occasionally, electrical gauging devices are also utilized for this purpose.

Optical Measuring Method

The scales used to measure the table's movement are safely enclosed within the machine to protect them from damage or wear. The table's motion is controlled through either a leadscrew mechanism or hydraulic systems. The table's position along both axes is determined by reading the scale visible through a microscope.

2.4. Applications of Jig Boring Machine

Following are the applications of the jig boring machine:

- For producing the pilot hole.
- For fabricate compound and progressive dies.
- Used to drill holes in jig bushing.
- The jig borer is frequently utilized for the production of jigs, fixtures, and dies, as well as for creating bushing holes for grinding and processing hardened components.
- Also used in alignment post in stripper or die set.

2.5. Moulding

Moulding is a manufacturing process used to shape materials, particularly plastics, into specific forms by using a rigid frame or mould. The process involves the application of heat and pressure to a material to achieve the desired shape. Moulding is a fundamental technique in the plastic industry and is essential for producing a wide range of plastic products, from simple containers to complex automotive components.

Steps in moulding process

1. **Material Preparation:** The raw material, typically in the form of pellets, powder, or resin, is prepared for the moulding process. This material is often plastic but can also include other substances such as rubber or metal.

2. **Heating:** The material is heated until it becomes pliable or molten. The heating method and temperature depend on the type of material and the moulding process used.
3. **Mould Filling:** The heated material is introduced into a mould cavity. Depending on the process, this might involve injecting, compressing, or blowing the material into the mould.
4. **Cooling:** The mould is cooled to solidify the material into the desired shape. Cooling times vary based on the material and the thickness of the part being produced.
5. **Ejection:** Once the material has solidified, the mould is opened, and the finished part is ejected. The part may undergo additional finishing processes such as trimming, painting, or assembly.

Advantages:

- **Versatility:** Capable of producing a wide range of shapes and sizes.
- **Efficiency:** High production rates, particularly with automated processes.
- **Precision:** Ability to create complex and detailed parts with high accuracy.
- **Material Utilization:** Efficient use of materials, with minimal waste.

Limitations:

- **Initial Costs:** High upfront costs for mould design and production.
- **Cycle Time:** Some processes have longer cycle times, affecting production speed.
- **Material Constraints:** Certain materials are better suited for specific moulding processes.
- **Design Restrictions:** Complex designs may require specialized moulds, increasing costs and production time.

2.6. Plastics

Plastics are a type of synthetic material that is manufactured using polymers. Polymers are complex molecules that consist of repeating structural units known as monomers. The aforementioned materials possess exceptional versatility, as they are capable of being moulded into a variety of shapes. Plastics can be also defined as organic materials which can be moulded or formed to shape by the application of pressure at moderate high temperature. Additionally, they exhibit a lightweight nature and a remarkable level of durability, rendering them indispensable in contemporary society. Plastics find extensive utilization across various industries, including packaging, construction, automotive, and electronics. Plastics are engineering materials offer the following advantages.

1. Plastics are much lighter in weight, strength -to-weight ratio of plastics can meet the requirement of many products.
2. They can be produced in a wide range of colours and shades, and can be processed easily.
3. They possess excellent electrical and thermal properties
4. They used as corrosion resistance materials to prevent from rust

However, the major limitations of plastics are:

1. Low strength and stiffness, and these properties are affected by temperature
2. Absorb moisture, and not dimensionally stable over a period of time

2.6.1 Types of plastics

Plastics can be broadly categorized into two main types on the basis of their physical properties:

1. **Thermoplastic plastics**
2. **Thermosetting plastics**

1. Thermoplastic plastics

Thermoplastic plastics softens under the application of heat and may be moulded under pressure. The shape is retained only after cooling i.e., thermoplastics softer when heated regain its hardness on cooling. During heating and cooling no chemical change occurs, and the parts produced can be reheated to change their shape.

The major thermoplastics materials are PVC (polyvinyl chloride), polythene, polypropylene, polystyrene, ABC plastics (acrylobutadiene styrene), cellulose acetate and nitrate, polytetrafluory ethylene (PTFE).

2. Thermosetting plastics

Thermosetting plastics are heated to render them plastics, and moulded under pressure. During heating, the materials undergo chemical change so that they can be moulded only once to form into rigid shape; that is, the materials will not soften if reheated. The major thermosetting materials are phenol-formaldehyde, polyesters, epoxy resins, alkyd resin, polyurethanes etc.

The difference between thermoplastics and thermosetting plastics are illustrated in Fig. 2.4 (a) and (b).

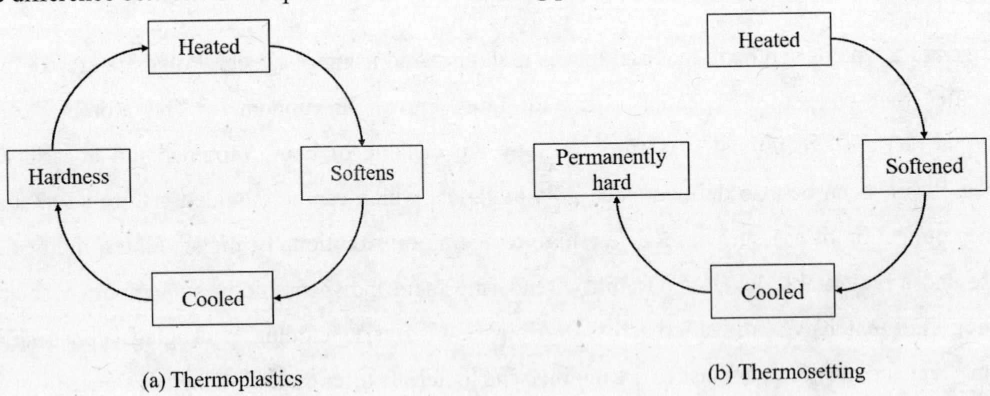

Fig. 2.4. (a) Thermoplastic plastic (b) Thermosetting plastics

2.7 Forming and shaping of plastics

The processing of polymers or plastics typically consists of the following stages:

- Producing the polymer (plastic) in the form of powder, granules, or sheets.
- Shaping the polymer into the desired form.

During the first stage, suitable additives may be mixed with the polymer to ensure the final product achieves the desired properties. The second stage generally involves heating the polymer (whether in powder, granular, or sheet form) until it becomes soft, molding it into the required shape, and then cooling it to solidify.

For thermoplastics, plastic deformable state is attained at appropriate temperature, and for thermosetting plastics this state is attained before set or cure through chemical reaction. The shaping of the plastics may be accomplished by several techniques, and the choice will depend on the following factors:

- Quality of items required,
- Items size,
- Production rate of item,
- Requirements for holes, inserts, threads etc.,
- Type of material being used.

2.8 Processing of plastics

Plastics can be processed to their final shape by a large number of different processes. However, the following methods are mostly used for processing the plastics.

- ❖ Moulding:

  (i) Compression moulding *(ii) Transfer moulding*

  (iii) Injection moulding *(iv) Blow moulding*

- ❖ Extrusion
- ❖ Thermoforming
- ❖ Calendering
- ❖ Casting

2.8.1 Moulding technique

Moulding is usually defined as the process of shaping of plastic material by the simultaneous application of heat and pressure or pressure alone in a closed chamber called the mould. The process offers the following advantages and limitations.

Advantages:

1. Parts produced are fairly accurate with a good surface finish.
2. Parts can be produced in a wide range of colors.
3. High production rate results in low unit cost.

Limitations:

1. High initial tooling cost.
2. Economical only for large production runs.
3. The shape and sizes of the parts are limited.

2.8.2 Injection Moulding

Injection moulding shown in Fig. 2.5 is used for moulding of thermoplastic materials. However, many reciprocation screw machines (Fig. 2.6) have the capability of handling thermosetting materials.

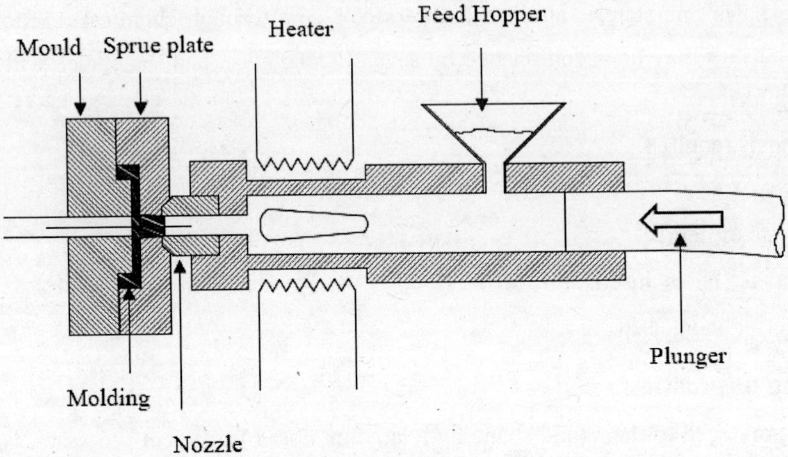

Fig. 2.5. Injection moulding (Ram type)

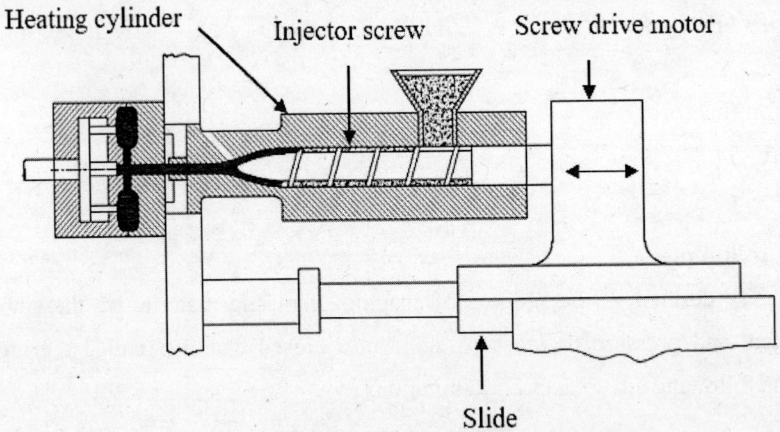

Fig. 2.6. Injection moulding (Screw type)

In this technique, a measured quantity of raw material is fed from the hopper into the chamber for each cycle. This charge is forced forward by the ram or screw into the heating chamber where its temperature is raised to about 150°C to 250°C, and pressure is built up to about 100 N/mm^2 to 150 N/mm^2; and then it is injected into the mould through a nozzle. The torpedo (spreader) increases the chamber temperature to allow faster moulding cycle. The mould is filled with plastic under high pressure. The pressure is maintained for a few seconds so that parts become rigid. Further the cooling is allowed (in the mould) before the mould is opened and finished articles are ejected. The gates connecting the product to sprue are removed.

Injection moulding can produce complex shapes with inserts, threads, holes, etc. and the rate of production is high. The process is particularly suitable for small parts such as knobs for electronic equipment, tool handle, pipe fittings etc. It is a high-rate production process will good dimensional control. Injection molding for thermosetting plastics is known as jet molding. In this process, the mold is maintained at a high temperature to facilitate hardening. The heating chamber is kept at a moderate temperature to prevent the plastics from hardening prematurely, while the nozzle is heated to a high temperature during the injection phase.

2.8.3 Compression Moulding

The compression moulding is widely used for thermosetting plastics. However, it is also applicable to thermoplastic materials. This process involves forcing a measured quantity powder or the preform, into the mould. The mould is closed and then heated, which softens the plastic to such an extent that it flows under pressure and completely the die cavity. The pressure is maintained till the plastic cured and becomes rigid. Thereafter the mould is opened and a part ejected from the mould cavity. In case of thermoplastic, the hardening is affected by chilling the mould while still under pressure. After cooling the parts are removed from the mould. However, thermosetting plastics can be removed without cooling the mould. The parts may be visually inspected and any flash is trimmed off. The principle of compression moulding is illustrated in below Fig. 2.7 (a) (b) (c)

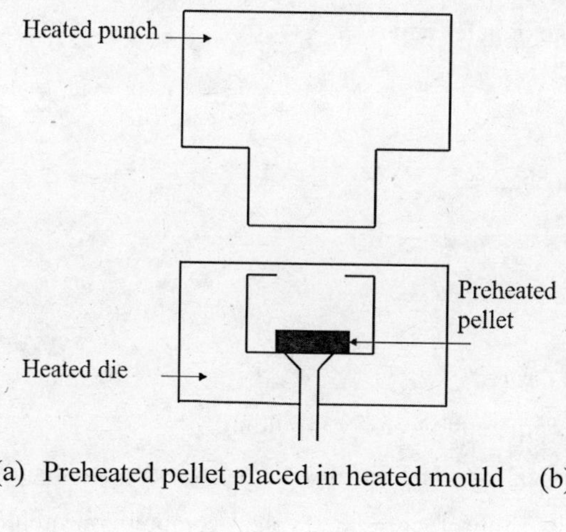

(a) Preheated pellet placed in heated mould

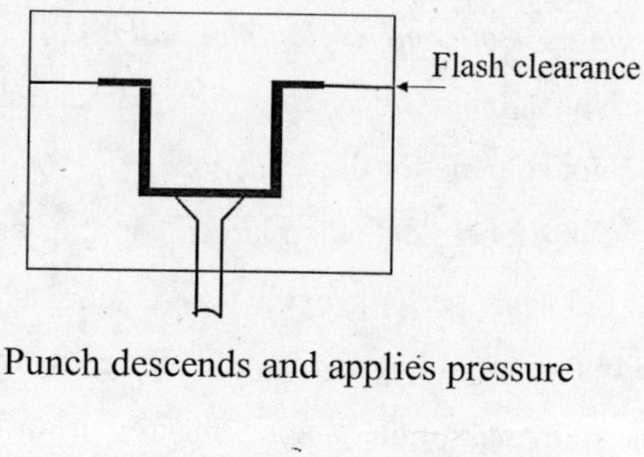

(b) Punch descends and applies pressure

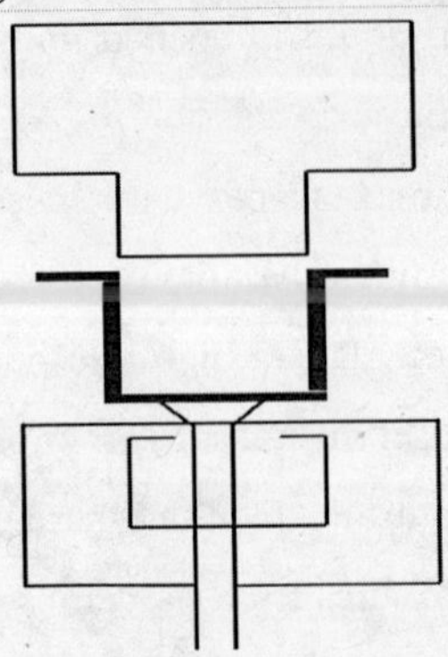

(c) After cooling part removed from the mould

Fig. 2.7. Compression moulding

The time taken for moulding cycle (all the steps beginning with charging the mould cavity and ending with ejection of parts) is referred as cycle time. The cycle time depends on the type of plastics, mould temperature and pressure, thickness of the section and the cooling rate. The moulding cycles for thermosetting plastics may take from 15 to 30 seconds for thin-walled parts and 1 to 5 min. for average parts. Moulding temperatures usually range from 120°C to 175°C, and pressure from 30 N/mm^2 to 50 N/mm^2. The moulding cycle for thermoplastics may takes one hour or more depending on the thickness.

Advantages of compression moulding:

1. Mould is simple and easy to make
2. No wastage of raw materials due to absence of gates and riser
3. Suitable shallow components having no inserts
4. Accuracy and surface finish are good
5. Parts with more uniform properties can be obtained

Disadvantages of compression moulding:

1. Not suitable for castings with intricate shapes.
2. Not suitable for thick sections.
3. Not economical when large quantities are desired
4. For same part, the cycle time is more as compared to transfer moulding

Compression moulding is most economical for small production runs. The process is most suitable for parts having simple shapes, but requiring high impact strength. Typical compression moulding parts include gaskets, seals, automotive panels, handles, container caps, fitting and washing machine housings.

2.8.3.1 Types of compression moulding

Depending upon the design, the compression moulding classified into following types:

1. Positive type, 2. Semi-positive type 3. Flash type

1. **Positive type**: In the positive type, the plunger fits tightly in the mould. In this case the amount of charge must be controlled closely to produce accurate size. Any variation in the amount of materials change into the cavity will result the variation of density in the parts produced.
2. **Semi-positive type:** In the semi-positive type, the plunger engages with a mould wall only during the last stage of its travel. In this case, excess materials can escape vertically until the plunger engages with the mould, and the charge does not have to be controlled very closely. Moreover, the vertical flash that results can be trimmed off easily. This this type of mould is suitable for deep mouldings and best suited for mass production of high-quality products.
3. **Flash mould:** This is simple type of mould. In this case the mould cavity is charged with slightly more material than is needed to produce the finished products, and the excess is squeezed out around the cavity in a thin flash. In flash moulding some materials and all components must be trimmed.

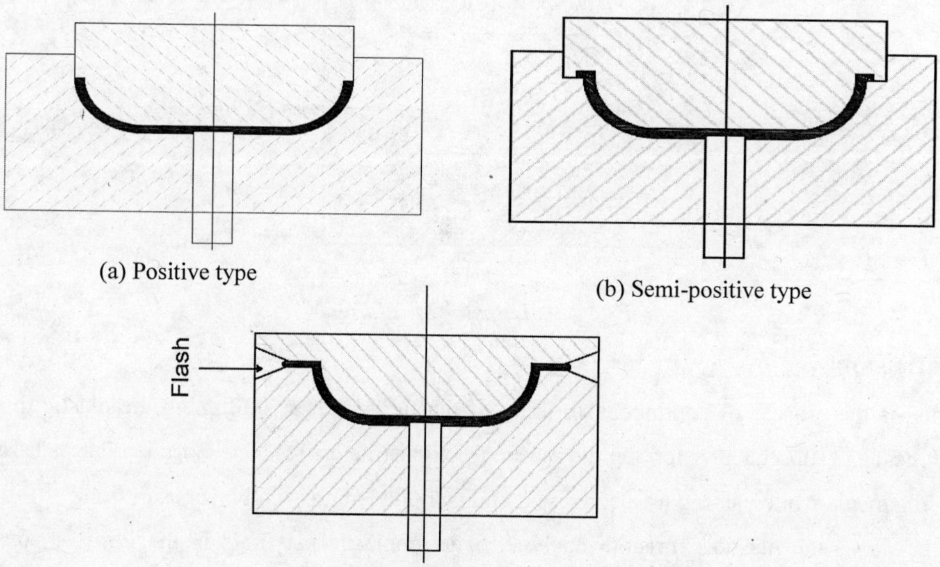

(a) Positive type

(b) Semi-positive type

(c) Flash type

Fig. 2.8. Types of compression moulding

2.8.4 Transfer Moulding

In transfer moulding (Fig. 2.9), the plastic powder is heated and pressed in a separate chamber (plasticising pot or the transfer pot) and then transferred through a gate (by a ram) into a closed mould which is maintained at high temperature. The material enters the mould at high pressure (70 N/mm^2) and cured at about 125°C to 175°C. In closed mould the plastic attains its shape and cured.

In transfer moulding the inserts can be more easily used than compression moulding and also finer details may be achieved. The mould is costly, but more uniform density and high mechanical strength in the products can be obtained. The mould is costly, but more uniform density and high mechanical strength in the products can be obtained. The other advantage of transfer moulding is that the change flow more readily permitting to produce large and intricate parts in a shorter cycle.

The process is suitable for thermos-setting plastics. Typical parts made by transfer moulding are electrical components and is particularly suitable for intricate shapes having varying wall thickness. Mould tends to be more expensive than those compression moulding and materials is wasted in the channels during filling.

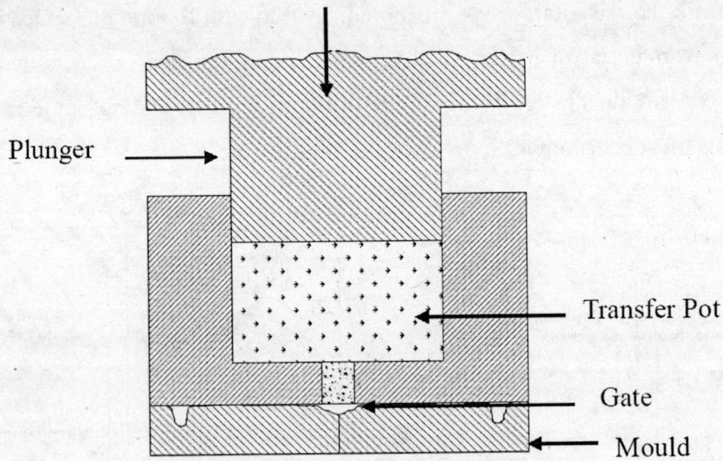

Fig. 2.9. Transfer Moulding

2.9 Extrusion

Extrusion is the process of continuous forming of plastic articles by softening the plastic material through heat and subsequently forcing the plastic through a die orifice. The extruded Part is hardened by cooling media while passing on a conveyor, and then the lengths can be cut as desired.

Fig. 2.10 shows the plastic extrusion machine. Thermoplastic materials in the form of power or pellets are fed into a heated cylinder through a hopper. Depending upon the material, the plastic being extruded is headed from 120° to 315° C. The headed plastic is forced into die orifice by the screw feeding mechanism.

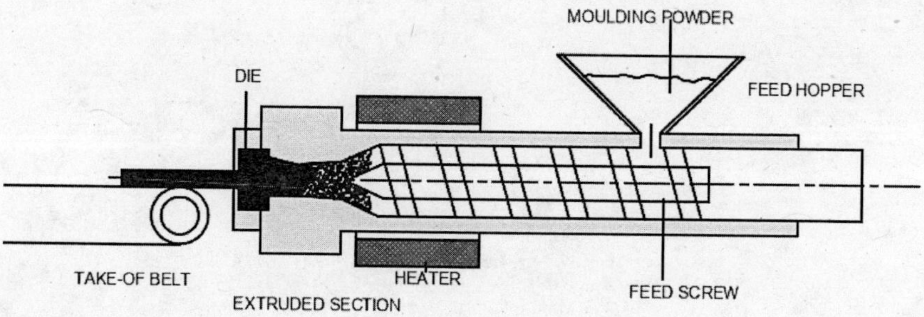

Fig. 2.10. Extrusion of plastics

The materials used in extrusion are polyethylene, PVC, ABC and polystyrene. Rods, tubes, strips and other forms of unform cross-section can be extruded. Intricate shapes can be produced and high output rate is possible. The products can be extruded in the wide range of colours offered by thermoplastics. The surface finish is good, and does not require costly finishing operations.

2.10 Casting

The low-viscosity plastics (polyester and epoxy resins) are convenient for casting operations. The process consists of pouring plastics, in liquid form, into the mould without pressure. After solidification plastic products are stripped from the mould.

Slush moulding: In slush molding, a thermoplastic resin slurry is introduced into a preheated mold. The heat from the mold causes the slurry to form a viscous layer, creating the desired wall thickness. After a specific period, the excess material is drained out. Upon solidification, the polymer product can be stripped from inside of the mould. The outside surface of the article reproduces the mould details to a high degree of accuracy. The slush moulding is used of manufacturing toys and thin-walled products such as gloves, insulated overshoes, artificial flowers and balls.

2.11 Calendering

Calendering is a process of continuous formation of thin sheets by squeezing a thermoplastic material between rolls. In this process, three or four heated rolls in a single stand are used to give a product of uniform thickness. The principle of calendaring is shown in Fig. 2.11. The thermoplastic compound is forced between two or more counter-rotating rolls to produce thin sheets or films. These films are hardened by cooling. The product thickness generally ranges between 1.0 to 0.3mm but can be reduced further by subsequent stretching. Sheet product by this process is subsequently used in thermoforming.

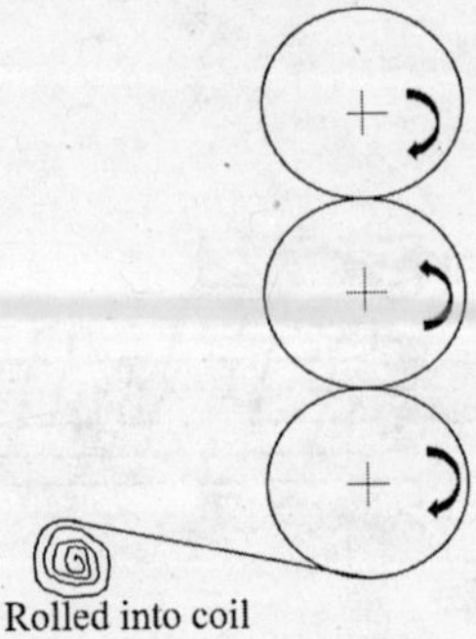

Fig. 2.11. Calendering

2.12 Blow Moulding

The blow moulding is for making hollow articles such as bottles from thermoplastics. The process involves placing the plastic in a cavity at plastic state (deformable state) and applying air pressure to blow into a shape. After allowing sufficient time for plastics to cool, the mould is opened and the part is removed. In this process the air pressure required is between 274 kN/m^2 and 689 kN/m^2. Usually, the higher the pressure, better the surface finish of the blown items. The products obtained from blow moulding include water bottles, toys, ornaments, containers etc.

There are different techniques of blow moulding, however, the following methods are most common.

1. Direct blow moulding, and 2. Indirect blow moulding.

1. Direct blow moulding: The process involves the extrusion of tube (parison) which is then clamped in a mould. Air is forced into the inside of the tube to blow the plastic to the shape of the mould. The mould is cooled to set the plastic. After cooling, the mould is opened and the part is removed. This process is sometimes referred as extrusion blow moulding. Fig. 2.12. shows the principle of direct blow moulding.

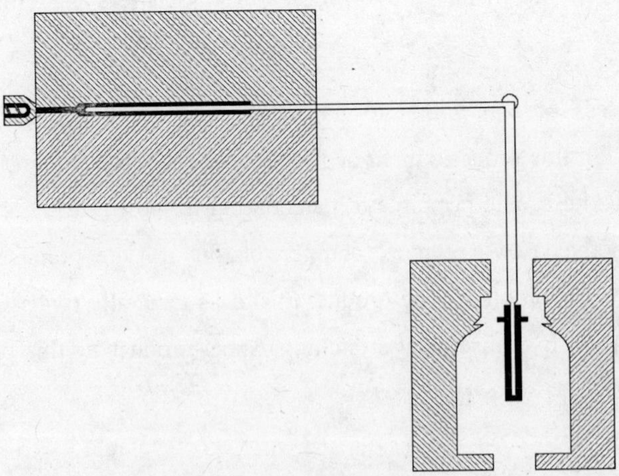

Fig. 2.12. Direct blow moulding

2. Indirect blow moulding: In indirect blow moulding, the air at high pressure is applied below the soft thermoplastic sheet. Under the air pressure the sheet is deformed into hemispherical shape. The principle of indirect blow moulding is shown in Fig. 2.13 (a) and (b).

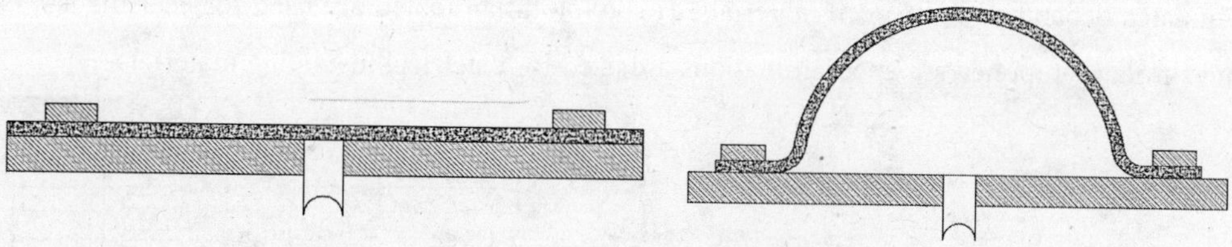

(a) (b)

Fig. 2.13. Indirect Moulding

2.13 Lamination and reinforcement

Laminates

Laminates are composite plastic materials made by layering paper, cloth, glass fiber, or nylon, which are then adhered using an appropriate resin. These products possess better properties such as tensile strength, impact strength, and improved resistance to corrosion. The laminates are available in the forms of sheets, rods, tubes. Major application of the plastic laminates includes components for mechanical and electrical equipment; and the plastic laminates include components for storage and handling of chemicals. Decorative laminates are used in the building and furniture industries.

Type of laminates:

1. Contact pressure laminations
   - ❖ Cured at a pressure of 0.2 N/mm^2.
2. Low -pressure laminations
   - ❖ Cured at a pressure of below 2.7 N/mm^2.
   - ❖ Low-pressure laminations are referred to as reinforced plastics.
3. High pressure lamination
   - ❖ Cured at 8 to 14 N/mm^2.

High pressure lamination process for sheets: The essential steps in the lamination process are described below:

1. The reinforcing material (paper, cloth, glass fibre, etc.) is passed though resin solution where it is impregnated with suitable resin. The commonly used resin for high pressure lamination includes phenolic, epoxy resins, polyesters, silicones.
2. The product is there passed though drier. The solvent is evaporated from the impregnated sheet by heating, leaving a fairly stiff sheet impregnated with plastic material. The whole process is continuous, as shown in Fig. 2.14.

3. The sheets are cut into convenient sizes. The desired number of sheets are stacked and the stack is placed between two highly polished sheets of steel. Pressure and heat are applied to achieve curing as desired. The finish on the steel surface is imparted to the laminated. The properties of laminates depend on reinforced materials. Heavy cloth laminated are used for gear blanks, cams and similar components; paper laminations are used for electrical insulating materials.

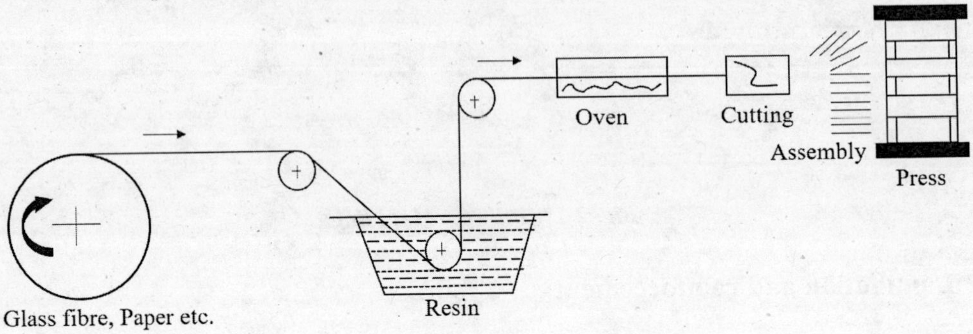

Fig. 2. 14. Manufacture of laminated sheets

2.13.1 Laminated tubes and rods

Laminated tubes are manufactured by tightly winding the resin-impregnated sheet onto a steel mandrel of the required diameter under pressure. This is achieved by rotating the mandrel between three large steel rollers, which apply pressure. The curing is done by heating a suitable oven, and after curing the material is removed.

Laminated rods are produced by wrapping resin-impregnated paper around a mandrel with the smallest feasible diameter. Before the curing process, the mandrel is removed, and the rolled material is transferred to a mold where the central hole is sealed. Heat and pressure are then applied to complete the curing process. The layout of equipment for manufacture of tube and rods is shown in Fig 2.15.

High-pressure laminated sheets, tube and rods are usually machined to get desired shape, size and surface finish.

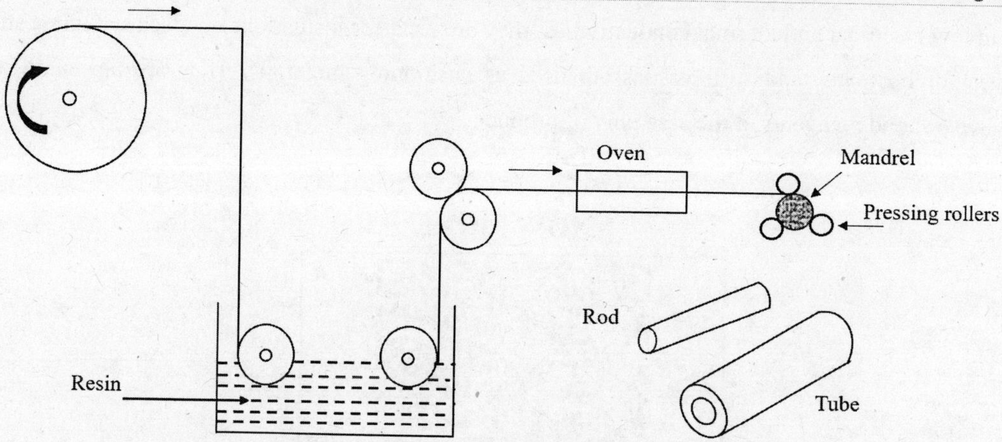

Fig. 2.15. Manufacture of tubes and rods

Low pressure laminating

Low pressure laminating is also called as reinforced plastic moulding includes several methods to produce products such as storage bins, loudspeaker horns, machinery housings and aircraft panels. In low pressure laminating, layers of the reinforcing material are placed in mould, and resin is sprayed on each layer. Fibre glass is most generally used reinforce material. Reinforced plastic mouldings may be cured under low pressure in vacuum bag or vacuum bag or pressure bag moulding. For accurate surface matched-metal moulding (closed moulding) method can be used; By proper distribution of the fibres, parts with uniform strength can be produced.

2.14 Plastics

Plastics can be defined as organic materials which can be moulded or formed to shape by the application of pressure at moderate high temperature. Plastics as engineering materials offer the following advantages.

- Plastics are much lighter in weight. Strength- to- weight ratio of plastics can meet the requirements of many products.
- They can be produced in a wide range of colours and shades, and can be processed easily.
- They possess excellent electrical and thermal properties.
- They can be used as a coating on steel to prevent corrosion

However, the major limitations of plastics are:

- Low strength and stiffness and these properties are affected by temperature.
- Absorbs moistures and not dimensionally stable over a period of time.

2.15 Applications of plastics

Plastics are utilized in applications where the material needs to endure low to moderate forces. Because of attractive colours and ease of fabrication, they are used for many packaging applications.

Due to low electrical and thermal conductivities, they are used for insulations on electrical wires and handles for hot pans, and soft plastics are used as cushioning materials. They are also used as adhesive or bonding agents in the assembly of products.

KNOW MORE

Plastic processing and technique

SUMMARY

Jig boring is a precision machining process performed on vertical milling machines to accurately position and size holes. Jig boring machines are specialized for high-accuracy operations and are categorized into open-front machines and cross-rail type machines. These machines are constructed with rigid frames, precision spindles, and accurate feed systems to ensure consistent performance. The system of hole location relies on precise alignment methods, such as templates, optical systems, or coordinate positioning, ensuring accurate placement and sizing of holes for critical components.

Further, in this chapter the processing of plastics involves various moulding techniques. Moulding processes include injection moulding, where molten plastic is injected into moulds for high-precision parts; compression moulding, which shapes plastic under heat and pressure; and transfer moulding, a variation where material is preheated before transfer to the mould. Extrusion involves forcing molten plastic through a die to create continuous shapes like pipes, while casting pours liquid plastic into moulds to solidify. Calendering is used for producing thin plastic sheets by rolling. Fabrication methods include sheet forming, blow moulding for hollow items like bottles, laminating plastics into sheets, rods, and tubes, and reinforcing to enhance strength. Plastics find applications across industries in packaging, construction, automotive, and consumer goods due to their versatility and durability.

EXERCISE

1. What are the advantages of plastics over other materials?
2. How is Injection molding done? State its advantages, limitations, and applications.

3. Explain the principle of the following processes with a neat sketch.
   (a) Blow molding
   (b) Extrusion
   (c) Tubes and rod manufacturing
   (d) Calendaring
4. Types of compression molding
5. State the advantages and limitations of injection molding.
6. Explain the system location holes.
7. Select suitable raw material and manufacturing process for any common plastic components giving reason.

   Ans:

Components	**Process**	**Raw materials**	**Reasons**
Bottles and other hollow container	Blow molding	Thermoplastics	Mold can be conveniently cooled to make the component rigid and hard
Tubes, Pipes and structural shapes	Extrusion	Thermoplastics in the powder or granular form	The component emerging from die is cooled easily by spray of water which hardens it to retain the shape
Electrical switch gear, parts that resist load and chemical attack	Transfer molding	Thermosetting plastics	High temperature and pressure maintained in the cavity promote curing which hardens the components

REFERENCES

1. Production Technology – HMT, Banglore, Tata Mc-Graw Hill.
2. Raghuwanshi, B.S., Workshop Technology, Vol II, Dhanpat Rai and Co, (2015).
3. https://ihshotair.com/blogs/resources/7-common-plastic-fabrication-methods-and-which-one-is-right-for-you?srsltid=AfmBOoo-vGk8R2Bd7JvnTn7hY6LuwSjeOT7pbPnmX_kaf3wfhTURsOgY

UNIT

3

MODERN MACHINING PROCESSES

UNIT SPECIFICS

This unit elaborately discusses the following topics:

- Introduction of modern machining process and comparison with traditional method
- Exploring the advanced machining process
- Description on output characteristics and controlling parameters of EDM and Wire EDM respectively

The establishment of a modern machining processes unit is a strategic decision driven by the increasing demand for high-precision, high-efficiency, and cost-effective manufacturing solutions across various industries. Traditional machining methods often fall short of meeting the precision, speed, and complexity requirements of contemporary industrial applications. Modern machining processes, such as ultrasonic machining, electrical discharge machining (EDM), wire cut EDM, abrasive machining, laser beam machining, and electrochemical machining, offer superior accuracy, automation, and material versatility, making them indispensable for industries like automotive, aerospace, medical devices, electronics, and defense. These advanced techniques enable the production of intricate components with minimal material wastage, reduced lead times, and enhanced durability. Establishing a modern machining processes unit not only caters to the growing demand for precision manufacturing but also creates opportunities for innovation, research, and sustainable production methods.

RATIONALE

The need for a modern machining processes unit arises from the increasing demand for high-precision, high-efficiency, and cost-effective manufacturing solutions across various industries. Traditional machining techniques often fail to meet the growing requirements for accuracy, speed, and complexity in industrial applications. In contrast, modern machining processes—such as ultrasonic machining (USM), electrical discharge machining (EDM), wire cut EDM (WEDM), abrasive machining, laser beam machining (LBM), and electrochemical machining (ECM) offer significant advantages in terms of precision, automation, and material adaptability. These advanced techniques are particularly crucial for industries such as automotive, aerospace, medical devices, electronics, and defense, where intricate components with tight tolerances are essential.

PRE-REQUISITES

Basics of production engineering and traditional machining processes

UNIT OUTCOMES

The list of outcomes of this unit is as follows:

U3-O1: Differentiate between traditional and modern machining processes.

U3-O2: Explain the construction and working of USM, EDM, WEDM, Abrasive water jet machining, LBM, ECM.

U3-O3: Realize about the machining characteristics of EDM.

U3-O4: Explain the performance parameters of WEDM.

Unit-3 Outcomes	Expected Mapping with Course Outcomes (*1- Weak Correlation; 2- Medium correlation; 3- Strong Correlation*)					
	CO-1	**CO-2**	**CO-3**	**CO-4**	**CO-5**	**CO-6**
U3-O1	2	2	2	2	3	1
U3-O2	3	3	3	1	3	3
U3-O3	2	3	2	1	3	3
U3-O4	2	3	2	1	3	3

3.1 Introduction

This chapter highlights non-traditional machining methods that excel in handling complex shapes, hard materials, and micro-machining with high precision. Techniques like Ultrasonic Machining, EDM, Wire Cut EDM, Abrasive Jet Machining, Laser Beam Machining, and Electrochemical Machining offer unique advantages for industries such as aerospace, automotive, and electronics, enabling intricate, versatile, and high-precision manufacturing.

Over the decades, throughout the global market, there is a continuous struggle for the economical production of products with better quality. This can be achieved only through optimal utilization of materials, resources and production methods. Apart from this, with the advancement in technology, scientists and engineers in the field of manufacturing are facing challenging problems requiring the development of newer and better methods of production. This has attracted the attention of many researchers to produce an effective product by removing materials from the raw component using certain developed new technical processes.

However, it has been known that material removal processes are mainly classified into conventional and non-conventional machining processes. Briefly, in conventional machining processes such as turning, milling, drilling, grinding, etc. the material removal takes place by applying only mechanical forces on the workpiece material through a cutting tool. During the past years, the conventional machining has been met the requirements of the industries. But in today's competitive industries, the stringent designers' requirements for products with higher economic production rates and better quality were imparting much more pressure on the capabilities of conventional processes to achieve the same.

Further, many problems have also imposed during the machining of new exotic materials such as super alloys, carbides, ceramics, etc. with ever-increasing mechanical properties by conventional means. Therefore, to meet these challenges, modern machining (non-traditional machining) processes has developed and established in the industry as efficient and economic alternatives to conventional ones. Additionally, these modern machining processes have become significant for complexity of workpiece surface shape and size, surface integrity and miniaturization requirements. Table 3.1 shows the comparison between traditional and modern machining processes.

Table 3.1: Comparison between traditional and modern machining processes.

Traditional Machining	Modern Machining
There is a physical tool contact (contact machining)	Usually no physical tool contact (non-contact machining)
Cutting tools must be harder than the workpiece	Machining of workpiece takes irrespective of its hardness and mechanical properties
Lower accuracy and surface finish	Higher accuracy and surface finish
Difficult to difficult materials cannot be easily machined	Difficult to difficult materials can be easily machined
Due to surface contact and wear tool life is decreases	Tool life is more
Lower capital cost	Higher capital cost
Easy to install	Complex experimental setup
Wastage of material is more	Wastage of material is less

Modern machining processes involve material removal from the workpiece through mechanical force, thermal energy, or electrochemical/chemical reactions. Table 3.2 categorizes these processes based on the type of energy and material removal mechanisms employed. Non-traditional machining methods are varied and are distinguished by their unique characteristics, modes of operation, and areas of application.

Table 3.2 Classification of non-traditional machining processes.

Type of energy	Material removal mechanisms of	Energy source	Process
Mechanical	Erosion	Mechanical motion	Ultrasonic Machining (USM)
		Pneumatic	Abrasive Jet Machining (AJM)
		Hydraulic	Water Jet Machining (WJM)
		Hydraulic	Abrasive Water Jet Machining (AWJM)
Thermal	Fusion and vaporization	Electric spark	Electrical Discharge Machining (EDM)
		High speed electrons	Electron Beam Machining (EBM)
		Powerful radiation	Laser Beam Machining (LBM)
		Ionized substance	Ion Beam Machining (IBM)
		Ionized substance	Plasma Arc Machining (PAM)
Electrochemical	Ion displacement	Electric current	Electro-Chemical Machining (ECM)
Chemical	Corrosive reaction	Corrosive agent	Chemical Machining (CHM)

3.2 Ultrasonic Machining (USM)

Ultrasonic Machining (USM) is an advanced machining technique (non-traditional) that removes material from a workpiece by combining high-frequency ultrasonic vibrations with abrasive particles. It is especially suitable for machining hard and brittle materials like ceramics, glass, and hard metals.

3.2.1 Construction of USM

The key components of a USM setup are as shown in Fig 3.1:

1. **Power Supply:**
   - Provides high-frequency electrical energy (typically 20–40 kHz) to drive the ultrasonic vibrations.
2. **Transducer:**
   - Converts electrical energy into mechanical vibrations.
   - Types of transducers include piezoelectric (common) or magnetostrictive.

3. **Tool Holder and Tool:**
   - The tool is mounted on the tool holder and is shaped to match the desired geometry.
   - The tool is made of a ductile material like stainless steel or brass.
   - It transfers the energy and, in certain situations, enhances the vibration's amplitude to achieve the desired effect.
4. **Abrasive Slurry:**
   - A mixture of abrasive particles (e.g., silicon carbide or aluminium oxide) suspended in a liquid like water or oil.
   - Acts as the cutting medium by impacting the workpiece surface.
   - Abrasive Particles have random sharp edges
5. **Nozzle:**
   - Directs the abrasive slurry to the machining area.

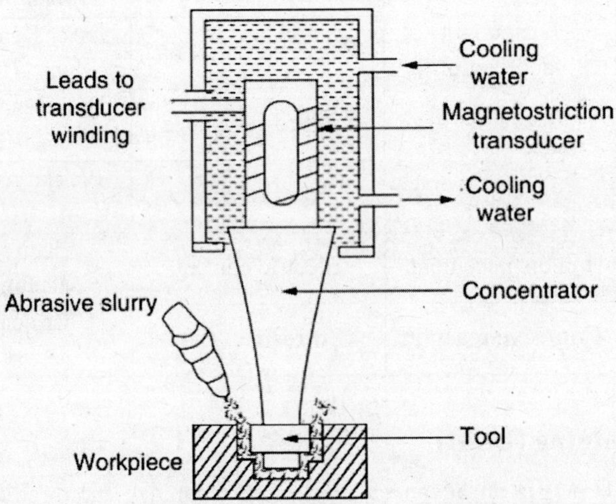

Fig. 3.1 Schematic of ultrasonic machining

6. **Workpiece:**
   - Must be rigidly clamped to prevent movement during machining.
7. **Vibration Amplifier (Horn):**
   - Amplifies the ultrasonic vibrations generated by the transducer and transmits them to the tool.

3.2.2 Working of Ultrasonic Machining

1. **High-Frequency Vibrations:**
   - The power supply generates high-frequency electrical energy.
   - The transducer converts this energy into mechanical vibrations, typically at a frequency of 20–40 kHz.

2. **Amplification and Transmission:**
    - The vibrations are amplified by the horn and transferred to the tool.
3. **Abrasive Slurry Action:**
    - The abrasive slurry is continuously fed into the gap between the tool and the workpiece through a nozzle.
    - The tool vibrates at a high frequency, creating a series of impacts on the abrasive particles in the slurry.
4. **Material Removal:**
    - The abrasive particles, propelled by the vibrating tool, strike the workpiece surface.
    - These impacts cause microscopic chipping or erosion, gradually removing material to form the desired shape.
5. **Tool Advancement:**
    - The tool is fed towards the workpiece under controlled pressure to maintain a consistent gap and ensure continuous machining.

3.2.3 Advantages of Ultrasonic Machining

- **Precision:** Capable of machining intricate shapes and fine details.
- **No Heat Generation:** Avoids thermal damage to the workpiece.
- **Versatility:** Suitable for hard and brittle materials like glass, ceramics, and carbides.
- **No Tool Wear:** The tool does not come into direct contact with the workpiece.

3.2.4 Disadvantages

- **Low Material Removal Rate (MRR):** USM is slower compared to traditional machining processes.
- **Tool Design Constraints:** Tool shapes are limited to simple geometries.
- **High Power Consumption:** Requires significant energy to generate ultrasonic vibrations.

3.2.5 Applications of Ultrasonic Machining

- **Electronics:** Machining of semiconductor materials.
- **Medical Devices:** Shaping hard materials like bioceramics.
- **Aerospace:** Precision machining of brittle composites and ceramics.
- **Jewellery and Glass:** Cutting intricate designs in glass and gemstones.

3.3 Electrical Discharge Machining (EDM)

Electrical Discharge Machining (EDM) was originated in the year 1770, when Joseph Priestly discovered the erosive effect of electrical discharges. But for a long period this area was not much discussed. In 1943, B.R. Lazarenko and N.I. Lazarenko have first given an idea of EDM process in which material removal takes place by controlled erosion through a series of electric sparks. Thereafter, research and development have brought this process to its present level.

Electrical Discharge Machining (EDM) is a thermo-electric process used to remove material from a workpiece (usually the anode) and a tool (the cathode) through a series of electrical sparks. These sparks occur at high frequency while both electrodes are immersed in a dielectric fluid. The process removes material by melting and evaporating it, with the debris being effectively cleared away. EDM is a vital technique in modern manufacturing, offering efficient material removal rates, the ability to produce complex and precise features, and minimal impact on the material's properties.

3.3.1 Principle of EDM

The basic schematic representation of EDM is shown in Fig. 3.2, and the corresponding ideal voltage and current characteristics waveform is shown in Fig. 3.3. In addition, the material removal mechanism in EDM is illustrated in Fig. 3.4.

At the beginning, a voltage difference (i.e. open circuit voltage, V_o) is applied between the tool (cathode) and workpiece (anode), submerged in a dielectric fluid and are separated by a narrow gap, known as spark gap/gap width. The capacitor is charged through resistance from the applied voltage. As long as the voltage in the capacitor is not reaching the breakdown voltage of the dielectric fluid under the prevailing machining condition, capacitor would continue to charge up to the duration of t_c (Fig. 3.3). This duration is known as charging time/off time/pulse interval. Once the breakdown voltage (V_b) is reached as shown in Fig. 3.3, an electrostatic field of sufficient strength is established across the two electrodes, causing emission of electrons from the cathode (Fig. 3.4 a).

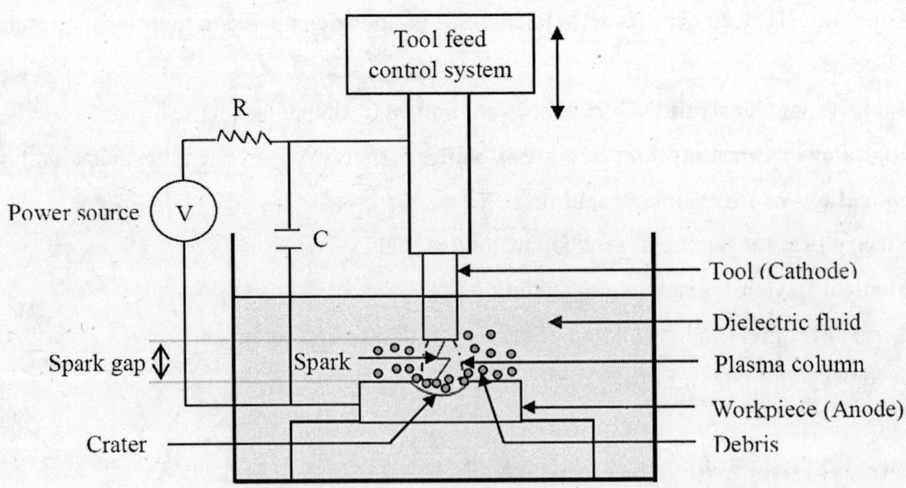

Fig. 3.2 Schematic representation of EDM.

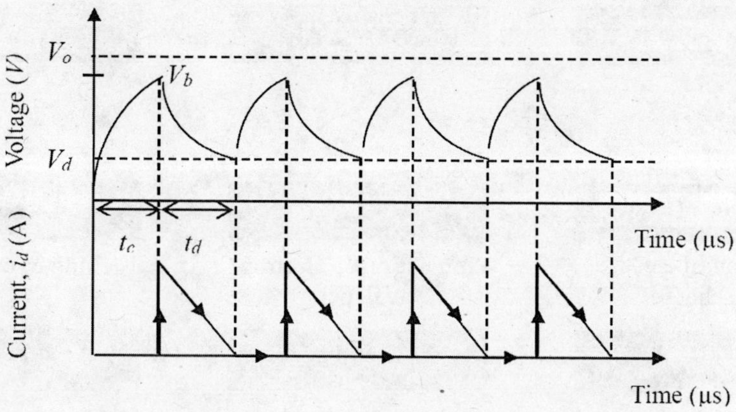

Fig. 3.3 Voltage and current characteristics waveform.

The released electrons accelerate toward the anode, and as they gain sufficient velocity, they collide with neutral atoms or molecules in the dielectric fluid, causing them to break apart into electrons and positive ions. These newly generated electrons also accelerate and may dislodge additional electrons from the dielectric fluid molecules. As a result, the insulating properties of the dielectric fluid deteriorate. Eventually, a narrow, ionized column of dielectric fluid, known as a plasma column, forms between the electrodes.

Since the electrical resistance of the plasma column is very less, all of a sudden a large number of electrons will from tool to the workpiece and ions from workpiece to the tool (known as avalanche of electrons), shown in Fig. 3.4 (b). At this point, the current (i_d) starts to discharge across the electrodes; the open circuit voltage drops to the discharge voltage (V_d) and the current (i_d) rises to its peak, as shown in Fig 3.3. Such a phenomenon can be normally seen as spark discharge. However, the spark discharge can takes place up to the duration of t_d, known as discharge time/pulse on time (Fig. 3.3). This indicates that the current continues to flow until almost all the energy is drawn out of the capacitor, at which time the current stops and again charging of the capacitor continues.

As a result of this spark, a very high temperature (of the order of 10,000-12000 ^{0}C) is produced at a localized spot on the electrodes where their surfaces are closest. This high temperature causes the melting and evaporation of the electrode materials (Fig. 3.4 c). Thus, material is removed in the form of debris or tiny solid material particles by thermally generated pressure wave leaving behind a small crater on both the electrodes surface (Fig. 3.4 d-e). At the same time, the debris are flushed away by the flow of dielectric fluid across the spark gap using dielectric recirculation system.

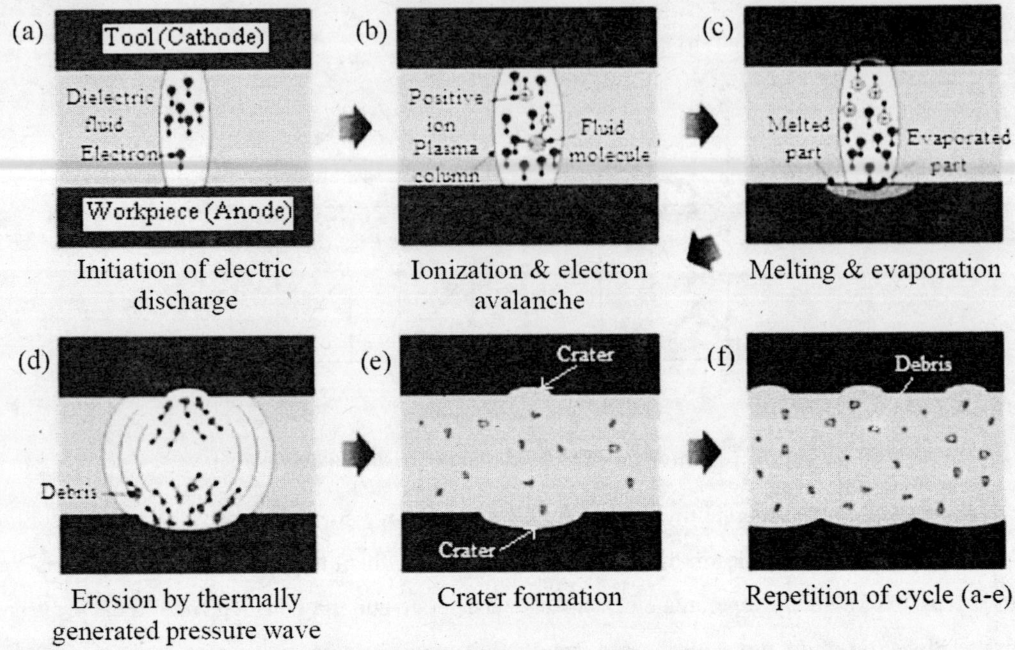

Fig. 3.4 Material removal mechanism in EDM.

As soon as this happens, the gap between the electrodes changes, necessitating the use of the tool. When the cycle is repeated, the sparks occur at different localized spots on the electrodes surface. This is due to the variation of local gaps attributed to the presence of asperities and irregularities on the surface of electrodes. So, the sparks get distributed all over the tool surface, leading to uniformly distributed material removal under the tool, and finally, the required feature is produced in the workpiece.

3.3.2 Salient Features of EDM

Some of the distinct features of EDM are as follow:

(i) EDM is a non-contact machining process i.e. machining can be done without applying pressure on the material, therefore eliminating mechanical stress, chatter and vibration problems.

(ii) It can machine any conductive material irrespective of their mechanical properties.

(iii) It facilitates the generation of three-dimensional complex features with the help of a solid tool and its associated motions.

(iv) It is capable of machining difficult-to-machine materials such as ceramics, carbides, super alloys, composites, heat resistant steels, etc.

(v) It is free from the complexities and implications of size effect that are involved in the use of conventional processes.

3.4 DESCRIPTION OF EDM EQUIPMENT

The basic components of EDM equipment are tool, workpiece, dielectric medium unit, pulse generation unit, tool feed control unit and X-Y stage control unit. Figure 3.5 shows these components of EDM system indicating different subsystems required to achieve controlled material removal process.

EDM process parameters, such as voltage, current, pulse frequency, pulse-on time, pulse-off time, duty cycle are set using pulse generation unit-based power supply. Tool feed control unit feeds the tool, maintaining a constant spark gap between the tool and the workpiece electrode to sustain spark discharges during machining. An X-Y stage control unit is used to achieve the relative position of the workpiece with respect to the tool for 3D machining. The debris generated during the EDM process are flushed away from the tool-workpiece interface by the dielectric fluid, and the fluid is filtered and recirculated back to the electrodes interface using dielectric circulation system or flushing unit.

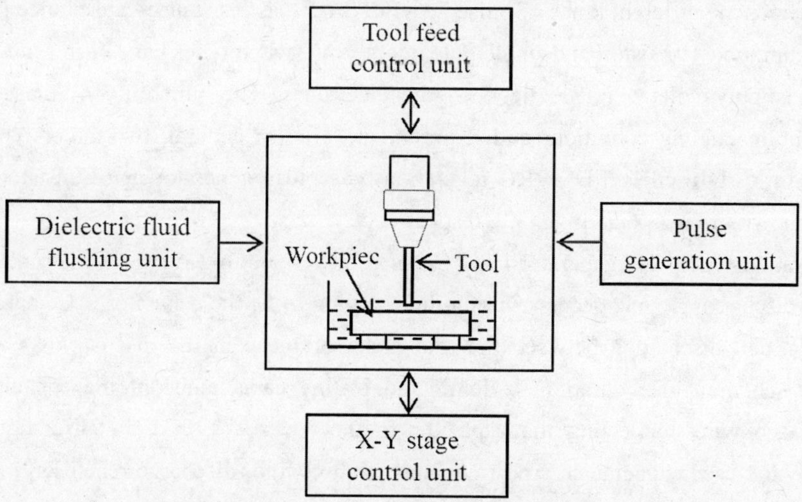

Fig. 3.5 Components of EDM.

A brief description of the components of EDM system is provided in the following section:

3.4.1 Tool and Workpiece Electrodes

The tool-electrode is responsible to transfer the electric current to the workpiece-electrode. The thermo-electric properties of the electrodes i.e. thermal and electrical conductivity, thermal expansion, melting and evaporation temperature have considerable effect on the material removal in EDM. In practical, the choice of the tool material mainly depends on the tool size, workpiece requirements, ease of machinability and cost.

The commonly used tool materials include Cu, Al, brass, Gr, Au, WC (tungsten carbide), copper-tungsten alloys, and silver-tungsten alloys. Similarly, workpiece materials often consist of Cu, Al, Ag, Gr, steel, superalloys, semiconductors, and ceramics.

3.4.2 Dielectric Fluid Flushing Unit

This unit consists of dielectric fluid, dielectric reservoir, pump to supply the dielectric fluid into the gap between tool and workpiece, filter to remove the debris/particles from the dielectric and to ensure recirculation of fresh dielectric to the machining zone. The dielectric fluid has several functions in the EDM process. But, in particular, the three most important functions are:

(i) It insulates the tool-workpiece gap (spark gap) and after breaking down at the appropriate applied voltages conduct the flow of current.

(ii) It flushes away the debris or particles generated in the spark gap.

(iii) It cools down the heated surfaces of the electrodes.

The most commonly used dielectric fluids are de-ionized (DI) water, kerosene, paraffin oil and transformer oil.

3.4.3 Pulse Generation Unit

This unit provides the pulsating direct current (DC) across the tool-workpiece gap. Based on the review by researchers, different kinds of pulse generators such as resistance-capacitance (RC), rotary impulse, vacuum tube, transistor, and single pole dual throw switch types have been found to be used in EDM that supply voltage pulses between the electrodes. The suitability of these generators depends on the machining conditions and requirements. But, in general, two major types of pulse generators are mostly used in EDM: RC relaxation-type pulse generator and transistor-type pulse generator as shown in Fig. 3.6 and Fig. 3.7, respectively.

In a RC relaxation-type pulse generator i.e. RC-based power supply (Fig. 3.6), the repetition of the charging and discharging cycle occurs. During the charging cycle the capacitor C is charged through the resistor R, and discharged between the tool and workpiece in the discharging cycle. In this circuit, the discharge pulse duration is dominated by the capacitance of the capacitor and the resistance of the wire connecting the capacitor to the electrodes, and the discharge energy is determined by the used capacitance. The frequency of discharge (discharge repetition rate) depends on the charging time, which is decided by the resistor used in the circuit. The current and gap voltage in this type of power supply is controlled at a predefined level throughout the pulse duration i.e. they are assumed to be maintained constant with time.

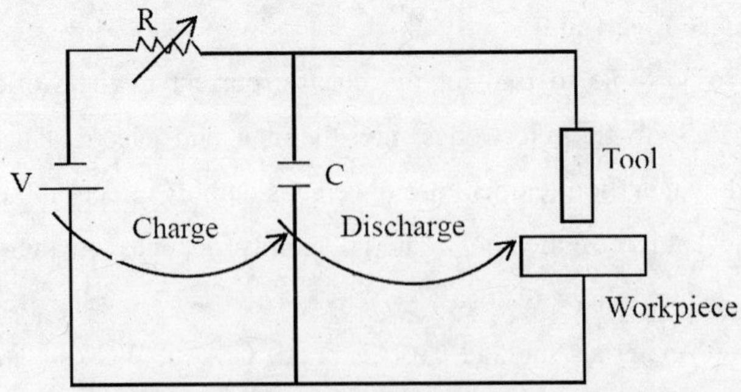

Fig. 3.6 RC relaxation-type pulse generator.

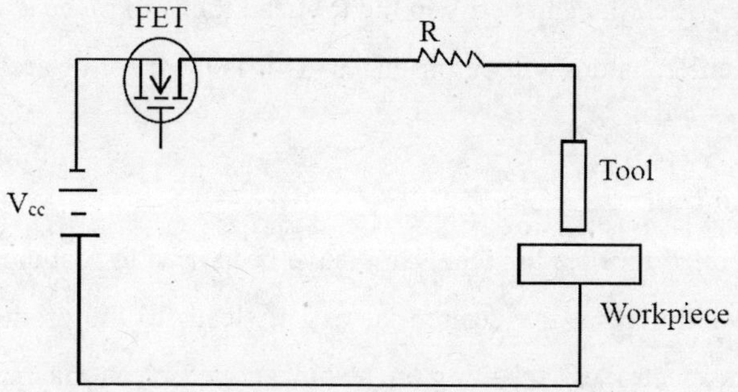

Fig. 3.7 Transistor-type pulse generator.

The RC relaxation-type pulse generator has been used especially where discharge current with high peak values and short duration is needed. But, with improved capability of power transistors that can handle large currents with high response, the transistor-based power supply shown in Fig. 3.7 replaced the RC-based power supply in EDM.

In a transistor-type pulse generator i.e. transistor-based power supply (Fig. 3.7), resistance and transistor are connected in parallel between the direct current power supply and the discharge gap. The Field Effect Transistor (FET) operates the switching on-off the gate control circuit. In order to generate a single pulse, the gap voltage is monitored to detect the occurrence of discharge and after the preset discharge duration, the FET is switched off. The discharge energy in every spark is controlled by the resistance (R) across the circuit and the input voltage (V_{cc}). Typically, in a transistor-type circuit the discharge current increases in proportion to the number of transistors, which are switched on at the same time.

Moreover, the pulse shape for EDM mainly depends on the type of pulse generator. The pulse shapes created by generators are usually rectangular, saw-tooth, square and trapezoidal, and have been developed for various functions. It was also noted that when a voltage pulse is supplied between the tool and workpiece using the pulse generators, the following five different types of events take place based on the gap conditions:

(i) **Open circuit condition:** This does not produce a spark and hence no material removal takes place from the tool and the workpiece.

(ii) **Short circuit:** Short circuit will occur when the tool physically touches the workpiece surface. This will result in high current flow and may damage the pulse generation and control circuit elements.

(iii) **Arc:** Arc will occur when the gap between the tool and the workpiece is less than the spark gap. Continuous arcs may lead to reduction in machining accuracy.

(iv) **Spark with higher delay time:** In this case, the actual gap is more than the spark gap, however, sparks will occur after some delay time which is more than the normal delay time for spark discharges. This may result in an increase in the machining time.

(v) **Normal sparks:** When the gap between the tool and the workpiece is equal to the spark gap, the spark of specified nature will be produced. This is the most desired sparking condition in EDM process.

3.4.4 Tool Feed Control Unit

In this unit, servo-controlled tool feed mechanisms have been used to maintain a constant spark gap between the tool and workpiece at the desired state. This leads to the production of normal spark discharges between the electrodes, resulting in stable and efficient machining during the EDM process. The commonly used servo-controlled tool feed mechanisms in EDM are servo motor, stepper motor, solenoid control and electromagnetic motor.

3.5 EDM PROCESS PARAMETERS

The major process parameters of EDM process are as follows:

- Open circuit, Breakdown and Gap voltage;
- Peak current;
- Pulse on time (T_{on});
- Pulse off time (T_{off});
- Duty cycle (D);
- Pulse frequency (f).

3.5.1 Open Circuit, Breakdown and Gap Voltage

Open circuit voltage is the critical ionization voltage below which there is no spark discharge and, therefore, no electric current flows between the tool and the workpiece. Breakdown voltage is the threshold voltage at which the initiation of breakdown occurs. However, when an ionization path is created through the dielectric, the current starts to flow. Thus, open voltage drops and stabilizes at the working gap level. This voltage at the gap between the electrodes is known as gap voltage.

3.5.2 Peak Current

Peak current is often used to indicate the highest current during the machining. However, in reality, during each pulse on time the current increases until it reaches a preset level, which is expressed as the peak current. From experimental evidences of past research work, it seems that the higher the peak current is, the higher will be the discharge energy. Accordingly, higher is the rate of material removal during the process.

3.5.3 Pulse on Time or Pulse Duration

This is the duration of time for which the current is allowed to flow per cycle. The main EDM operation is effectively done during this period. It is the work part of the spark cycle, when the current flows and work is done only during this time.

3.5.4 Pulse off Time or Pulse Interval

This refers to the time interval between two consecutive sparks when the discharge is inactive. The pulse-off time represents the pause needed for the dielectric to re-ionize. During this period, molten material solidifies and is flushed out of the spark gap.

3.5.5 Duty Cycle or Duty Factor

Duty cycle is a percentage of the pulse on time relative to the total cycle time. It is calculated in percentage by dividing the on time (T_{on}) by the total cycle time (T_{on} + T_{off}). Generally, a higher duty cycle means increased machining efficiency.

3.5.6 Pulse Frequency

Pulse frequency is the number of cycles produced across the spark gap in one second. It is the reciprocal of total cycle time.

3.6 OUTPUT CHARACTERISTICS OF EDM

The major output characteristics of EDM are as follows:

- Material removal rate (MRR)
- Tool wear rate (TWR)
- Overcut
- Taper cut
- Surface roughness

3.6.1 Material removal rate (MRR)

Material removal rate (MRR) is defined as the volume of material removed per unit time. It is the ratio of the difference of weight of the workpiece before and after machining to the machining time and density of the material.

$$MRR = (W1 - W2)/(t\rho) \tag{3.1}$$

$W1$ = weight of the workpiece before machining.

$W2$ = weight of the workpiece after machining.

t = machining time.

ρ = density of workpiece material.

3.6.2 Tool wear rate (TWR)

Tool wear is an important parameter that affects the dimensional accuracy and the shape of the feature produced. It is related to the melting point of the materials. TWR is the ratio of the difference of weight of the tool before and after machining to the machining timc.

$$TWR = (Wt1 - Wt2)/t \tag{3.2}$$

Wt_1 = weight of the tool before machining.

Wt_2 = weight of the tool after machining.

t = machining time.

3.6.3 Overcut (OC)

Overcut (OC) is the dimension by which the cavity in the workpiece exceeds the size of the tool electrode. The magnitude of the overcut is dependent on the spark length and to a certain extent, on the dimension of the crater. When the debris are present in the spark gap, the effective length of the spark is increased and thus, the magnitude of overcut increased by the diameter of the debris, as shown in Fig. 3.8 (a). Overcut found to be important when close tolerance components are required to be produced for space application and in tools, dies and moulds for press work (Ghosh and Mallik, 2010; Dewangan, 2010). As overcut is inherent to the EDM, it is not possible to prevent overcut. But the overcut can be compensated if proper tool design is carried out.

$$OC = (Dh - Dt)/2 \tag{3.3}$$

D_h = diameter of the hole machined in the workpiece.

Wt_2 = diameter of the tool.

3.6.4 Taper cut

When the top portion of the hole walls is subjected to many spark discharges than the bottom portion, then taper cut occurs (Fig. 3.8b). The taper cut can be controlled by an appropriate insulation of the tool electrode.

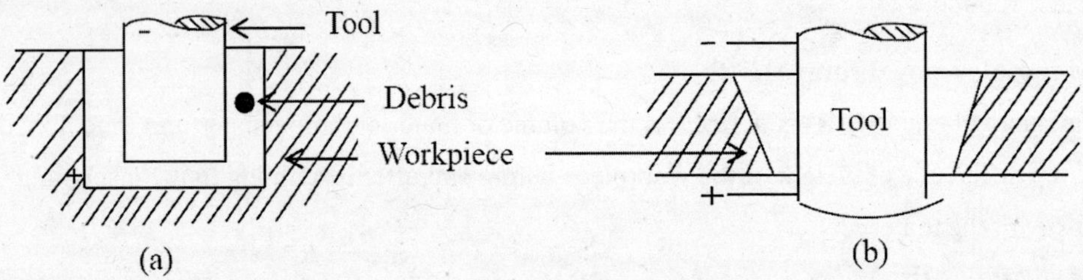

Fig. 3.8 (a) Overcut and (b) Taper cut.

3.6.5 Surface roughness

Surface roughness is defined as the irregularities present on the machined surface. In EDM, the surface roughness of the machined workpiece occurs due to the formation of craters (craters size/depth of craters) caused by the repetitive spark discharges. By controlling the crater size, which is mainly dependent on the energy per spark it is possible to control the surface roughness. This indicates that the surface finish can be improved by decreasing the energy of spark i.e. by decreasing working gap voltage, current and pulse duration. Further, the surface finish would be improved by forced circulation of the dielectric fluid.

3.7 APPLICATIONS OF EDM

EDM is capable of machining complex blind cavities, deep holes, and extremely complicated shapes on various engineering materials. As such, EDM has found widespread applications in many industrial domains, such as mold and die manufacturing, small and burr-free hole drilling in turbine blades, making spool valves and key ways for cylinders, etc.

3.8 WIRE ELECTRICAL DISCHARGE MACHINING (Wire EDM)

The wire EDM is one of the variants of EDM. The photographic view of the Wire EDM equipment (Model: ECOCUT ELPLUS15; Make: Electronica India Ltd., Pune) used to process the workpiece material is shown in Fig. 3.9. This setup comprises several components: a mount table, a wire supply system, a wire guide system, a wire collector bin, a filter storage tank, and a dielectric fluid supply. The mount table can adjust the position with a least count of 1 μm in both the X and Y axes, featuring dimensions of 370 mm × 600 mm, a workpiece height of 200 mm, and supports a maximum weight of 300 kg.

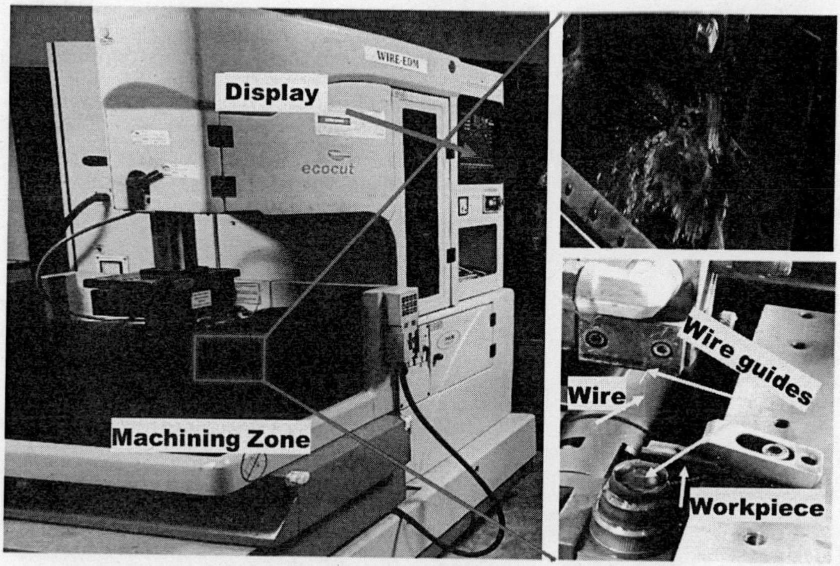

Fig. 3.9 Wire EDM equipment.

The worktable can be remotely controlled along the X and Y axes, enabling operations such as starting or stopping the machining process and modifying the movement speed of the worktable. The worktable is equipped with M8 threaded holes for securing the workpiece using clamps. The wire guide system includes guides that keep the wire properly aligned while the wire supply mechanism feeds the wire from the spool, maintaining consistent tension. The guideways, with a tolerance of 5 μm, come in various diameters that can be swapped according to the dimensional needs. The wire spool is affixed to the machine, unwinding as the cutting process advances. The dielectric fluid utilized is deionized water, and the machine contains a storage tank with a capacity of 140 liters. A filter system employing 10μ single cartridges is also incorporated. The wire collector bin is designed to gather the machined wire, which requires periodic emptying.

3.8.1 Principle of Wire EDM

The working principle of wire EDM is same as that of conventional EDM. It uses a traveling wire electrode that passes through the workpiece to machine the material instead of a tool electrode that slowly enters the workpiece. The wires are made of copper, brass, or molybdenum with diameters ranging from 10 microns to 500 microns, and the workpiece materials must be electrically conductive. Wire EDM operates on a thermoelectric principle, facilitating material removal from the workpiece through spark erosion within the machining zone. This process utilizes a wire as the electrode tool, which acts as a cathode, while the workpiece acts as the anode. Deionized water, employed as the dielectric medium, is continuously circulated in the machining zone through a nozzle. The wire and workpiece are linked to a DC power source, maintaining a consistent gap between them. This gap, often half the diameter of the wire, is called the spark gap. To feed the wire electrode through the workpiece, an initial hole must often be drilled in the workpiece prior to wire EDM. Figure 3.10 demonstrates the operational principle of the WEDM process There are three crucial components of WEDM, which include the following:

- Generator
- Servo system
- Dielectric system

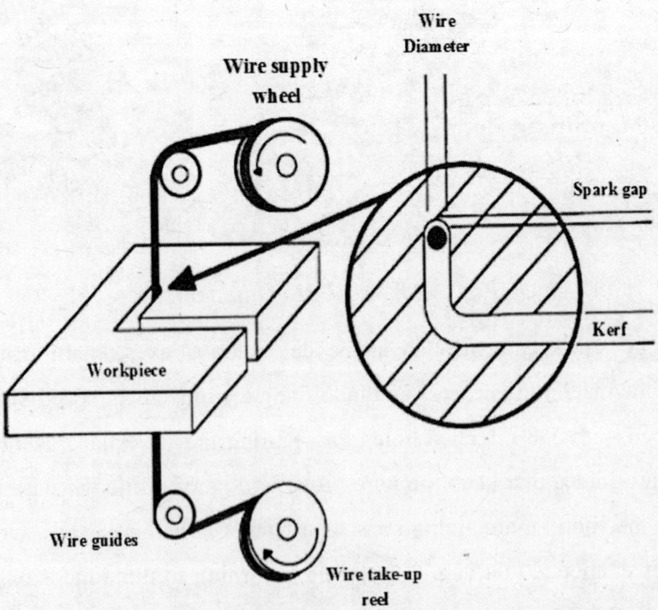

Fig. 3.10 Schematic diagram of Wire EDM.

3.8.2 Crucial Components of Wire EDM

3.8.2.1 Generator

In Wire EDM, applying electrical energy, which is delivered through short-duration impulses across the machining gap, is essential. This necessitates the use of specifically designed generators. The classification of generators used in spark erosion is determined by the method of voltage transformation, how control is implemented, and the discharge characteristics. Contemporary Wire EDM machines utilize controlled pulse generators, facilitating the adjustment of spark frequency and the intensity of the discharge. These pulse generators are invariably equipped with an electronic interrupter capable of handling high current flows.

3.8.2.2 Servo system

In Wire EDM, the distance between the cutting tool and the workpiece is managed by a servo system. This system operates based on the difference between a predefined reference voltage and the actual voltage across the separation. Upon detecting this variance, the signal undergoes amplification, leading to an adjustment of the tool's position by a hydraulic mechanism to compensate for wear. A short circuit within this space prompts the servo to adjust the tool's movement, ensuring the restoration of the appropriate separation. For effective utilization in Wire EDM, a servo system must exhibit several key characteristics:

- Precise positioning of the tool relative to the work surface.
- Sharp sensitivity to alterations in the separation conditions.
- Rapid responsiveness and the ability to sustain a consistent separation.

3.8.2.3 Dielectric fluid

In Wire EDM, deionized water is frequently chosen as the dielectric fluid due to its advantageous thermal characteristics, low viscosity, and ability to maintain a pollution-free environment. Additionally, deionized water presents no fire risk and possesses a high cooling rate, contributing to an increased MRR. The low viscosity facilitates an efficient flow, and the high cooling rate assists in producing a notably thin recast layer, making deionized water a preferred choice for this role. While deionized water is commonly selected, kerosene is another substance that can serve as a dielectric fluid in WEDM applications. For a fluid to be considered suitable for use in the WEDM process, it must meet several key criteria. They are:

- It should remain electrically insulating until a specific breakdown voltage is achieved.
- It should possess a high dielectric strength along with adequate fluidity, and
- It should be able to quickly extinguish or de-energize the spark or spark gap following discharges.

3.9 CONTROL PARAMETERS OF WIRE EDM

The control parameters of Wire EDM significantly impact the efficiency and control of the machining operation, facilitating an enhanced MRR and improved surface quality. The influence of

Wire EDM parameters on the machining outcomes necessitates a comprehensive discussion of each parameter's role. The following section outlines some critical parameters involved in the process:

3.9.1 Pulse-ON time or Spark time

The duration of spark permitted per cycle is referred to as the pulse-ON time. It is measured in microseconds (μs).

3.9.2 Pulse-OFF time or spark pause time

The interval known as the Pulse-OFF Time refers to the period between consecutive sparks in microseconds (μs). It should be noted that no voltage is present during this phase.

3.9.3 Servo or gap voltage

In Wire EDM, the servo voltage plays a crucial role as a process parameter. It communicates with the servo system through a gap voltage sensor, maintaining a specified distance between the tool and the workpiece.

3.9.4 Wire feed rate

The feed rate of the wire refers to the velocity at which the wire electrode progresses along the path of the wire guide, ensuring a consistent supply for sparking purposes. This parameter typically spans from 1 to 15 m/min.

3.9.5 Servo feed

The servo feed setting regulates the servo speed during machining. In normal feed mode, the servo speed adjusts in response to changes in gap voltage, whereas in constant feed mode, it remains fixed regardless of gap voltage fluctuations.

3.9.6 Peak current

The peak current (IP) represents the highest current that flows between the electrodes during a single pulse.

3.9.7 Wire distance between guides

The wire distance between guides, or the guide span, refers to the separation between the upper and lower wire guides during cutting operations, denoted by L as depicted in Fig. 3.11. It is important to note that the lower guide is fixed, while the upper guide is exclusively guided and moveable.

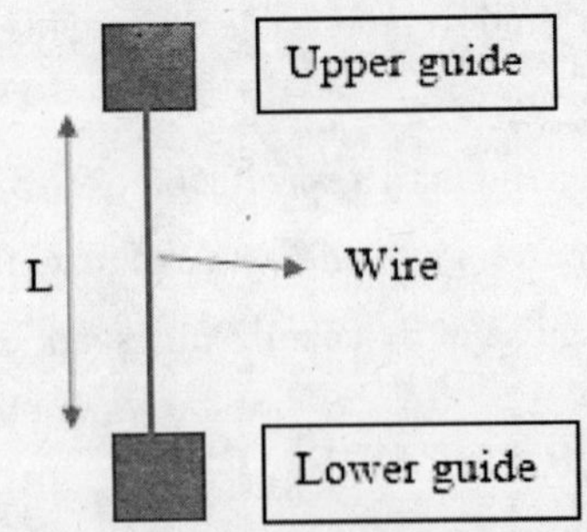

Fig. 3.11 Schematic illustration of the distance between the wire guides.

3.9.8 Corner dwell time (C-dwell time)

C-dwell duration refers to the interval during which the wire guide remains stationary at designated coordinates, awaiting the wire's arrival before proceeding with the subsequent instruction. This parameter is critical for attaining more precise angular definitions. The allowable adjustment range for this duration spans from 0 to 99 seconds. By default, the machinery is configured with a C-dwell duration of 3 seconds, which is the recommended setting for optimal performance.

3.9.9 Cutting speed over-ride

Adjusting the cutting speed override is a feature that reduces the cutting speed by a specific percentage, facilitating the maintenance of preset machining parameters during the machining process. This capability enhances the management of corner edges, supports the creation of larger taper angles in taper cutting, and aids in executing intricate profiling, thereby minimizing the likelihood of wire breakage. The adjustment can be made in various increments, including 25%, 50%, 75%, and 100% (indicating full cutting speed).

3.9.10 Wire offset

Wire offset refers to the predetermined parallel spacing allocated to the wire during the process of profiling a workpiece, serving the purpose of preventing excessive cutting. This parameter is crucial in establishing the tolerance levels of the profile. It is measured in micrometres, indicating the adjustment of the wire, either outward or inward, in a direction parallel to the intended profile.

3.10 APPLICATIONS OF WIRE EDM

Wire EDM can cut all types of ruled surfaces. This process can be used to cut the difficult-to-cut aerospace materials like titanium and Inconel alloys to any desired shape. It can fabricate very thin micro-EDM electrode with very higher aspect ratio.

3.11 ABRASIVE WATER-JET MACHINING (AWJM)

AWJM is a non-contact, inertia-less cutting process that has several benefits, including narrow kerf width, insignificant HAZ, and flexibility in material removal. Various kinds of abrasives are used in AWJM like garnet, olivine, aluminium oxide (Al_2O_3), silica-sand, glass bead, silicon carbide (SiC), zirconium, etc.

AWJM is a mixture of Abrasive flow machining and water jet machining. The removal of the material is through the erosion process. The erosion of the metal happens due to the high-force impact of the high-velocity jet of water along with the abrasive slurry. This process does not alter the metallurgical properties of the substrate as it is a non-thermal, non-electrical and non-chemical process. In addition, as this process mostly uses water as the jet fluid, the fluid itself acts as a coolant.

3.11.1. Working Principle

A highly pressurized flow of fluid is directed through a nozzle and a high velocity stream and a highly focused beam of fluid is used to abrade the material and hence cause material removal. The flow is assisted with abrasive particles to enhance the abrading action of the jet.

In AWJM process, water containing abrasive particles, which possess high velocity, is used to cut various materials ranging from soft to hard and ductile to brittle materials. Hard abrasive particles are accelerated in the cutting head by a high-velocity jet of water to accomplish the cutting of the material. The cutting head comprises an orifice, a mixing chamber, an inlet for abrasives, and a focusing tube. Water at pressures up to 400 MPa is made to flow through an orifice with a diameter ranging from 0.1mm to 0.3 mm, where a high-velocity jet of water is created. The velocity of the water jet is proportional to the square root of the water pressure and usually varies up to 1000 m/s. The high-velocity water jet is provided with the abrasive material through the abrasive inlet. The abrasive material will be mixed with the water in the mixing chamber, which is placed below the orifice. Abrasive particles are then made to accelerate in the focusing tube, whose diameter is usually twice that of the diameter of the orifice. During the suction of abrasive particles, air also enter through the abrasive inlet, and droplets start to generate around the jet and the abrasive particles are fragmented in the acceleration process. The resulting high-velocity jet consists of abrasive particles, water and air form the tool in the AWJM. Detailed parts of the AWJM cutting head is shown in Fig 3.12.

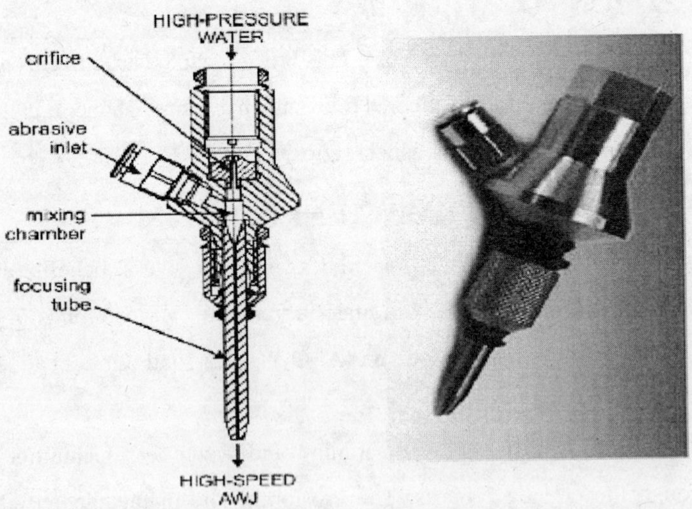

Fig. 3.12 AWJ cutting Head

The following figure 3.13 provides the schematic flow of the process. The fluid supply unit (water tank in the case of AWJM) provides the required fluid for machining, the mixing chamber mixes the abrasives with the fluid stream. Then the accumulator, which is a high-pressure pump and the pressure of the cutting fluid is increased in the intensifier unit. Then the programmed controls adjust the flow of the fluid mixture. The processed flow passes through the valve and then moves into the nozzle (mostly made of sapphire). The high pressure of the mixture is converted to a high velocity jet of fluid. This is directed onto workpiece in a pre-programmed path. Moreover, due to the abrading action of the fluid and the abrasives, the cutting action is achieved.

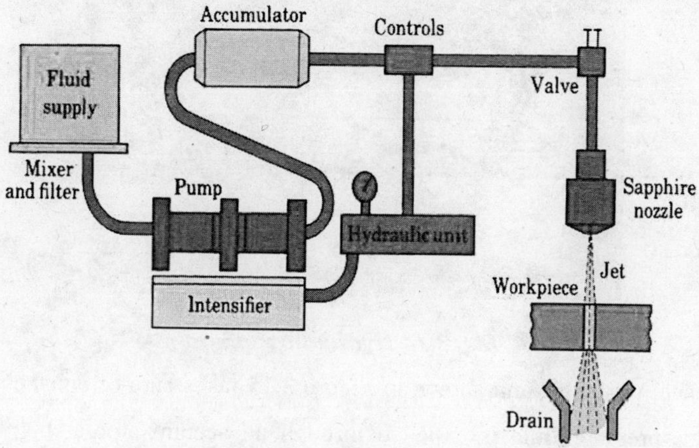

Fig. 3.13 Schematic of the AWJM process

3.11.1.1. Limitations

1. Form rough wavy patterns on the surface when the work matcrial is too thick because of the diverging action of the jet.
2. Dimensional inaccuracy while cutting a thicker specimen as the abrasive slurry jet gushes out at different angles when it enters the work piece.
3. Relatively low MRR in comparison to the LBM and WEDM process (when Heat Affected Zone is not critical).

3.11.1.2. Vital Components

The vital components of the Abrasive Water Jet Machine are

- Hydraulic Pump
- Intensifier
- Accumulator
- High-Pressure tubing
- Nozzle
- Orifice
- Control System
- Catcher tank or Drain

Hydraulic Pump: Hydraulic pump as shown in Fig 3.14, which helps in creating pressure in the fluid. This is driven by a high-speed electric motor. This is the main component of the system as a pump converts the mechanical rotation energy into the pressure energy of the jet. Hence, creating a high-intensified bean of water.

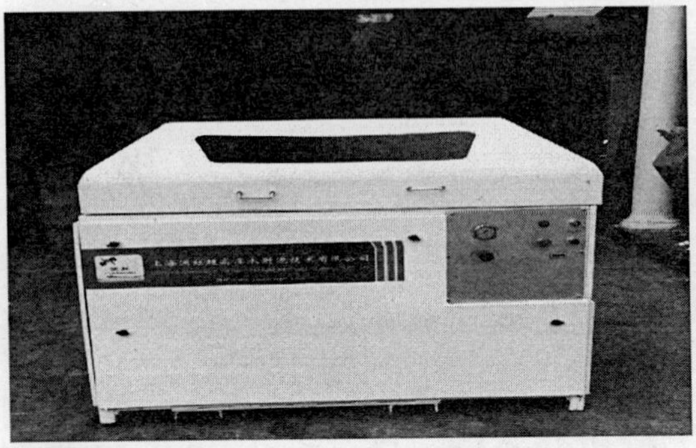

Fig. 3.14 Hydraulic Pump

Intensifier Unit: The intensifier unit shown in Figure 3.15 takes care of enhancing the pressure of the fluid. Here, low-pressure fluid is expelled through an accumulator at high pressure. This is handled by a hydraulic reciprocating mechanism.

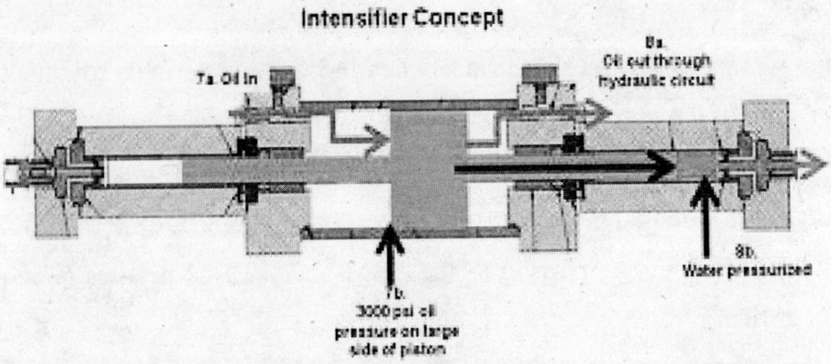

Fig. 3.15 Hydraulic Pressure Intensifier

Accumulator: As usual, the accumulator (in Fig 3.16) maintains the continuity of the fluid flow, eliminating pressure fluctuations. This system potentially helps the system during power cuts or in case of damage to the working system. This maintains the pressure and holds the system in stand still, such that when the power resumes, the cutting starts from the place where it is left.

Fig. 3.16 Accumulator Unit.

High Pressure Tubing: This acts as a bridge between the pressurized fluids in the accumulator to the cutting head. These tubes (Fig. 3.17) usually are made of tungsten or any other hard metals such that it resists abrasion caused from jet and abrasive particles.

Fig. 3.17 Tubing

Jet Pressure Nozzle: Here, the high-pressure jet is transformed to high intensity high-velocity jet. The main agenda of the AWJ nozzle (Fig. 3.18) is to offer effective mixing of the abrasives and the water-jet and to create high-velocity abrasive water-jet combination. A nozzle is a basic system, which works on the Bernoulli's principle. The nozzle mechanism shown in Fig. 3.19. The pressure energy at the inlet side is converted into kinetic energy in the orifice, which is present in the nozzle. The orifice converts high-pressure jet into high-velocity jet. The work of the AWJ nozzle is that it focuses the high-velocity beam.

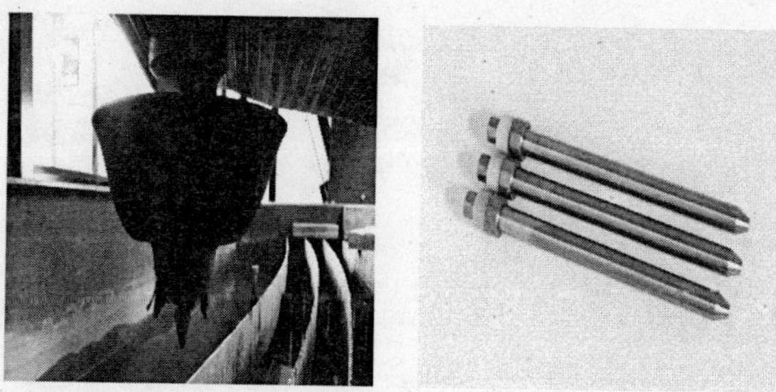

Fig. 3.18 Guide Nozzle

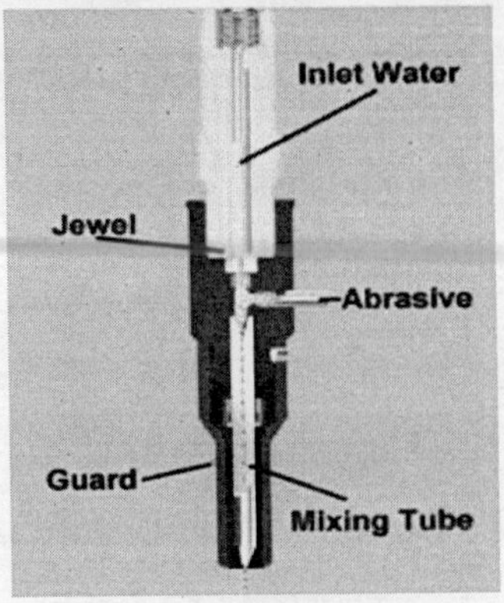

Fig. 3.19 Nozzle mechanism

Catcher tank: As shown in Fig. 3.20, a catcher tank is an arrangement of steel plates, which acts as the base of the substrate. This is mainly meant for debris collection and sound reduction. This acts as a cushioning to the impinging jet. This takes up the impact of the jet and prevents water and abrasives from wobbling out of the tank.

Fig. 3.20 Catcher tank

Factors Influential in the Abrasive Water Jet Machining:

Jet/ Nozzle based factor

- Nozzle Diameter
- Nozzle Length
- Orifice diameter
- Standoff distance

Jet fluid based

- Fluid type: mainly water or any other low viscous fluid.
- Fluid velocity
- Flow rate
- Flow Pressure
- Traverse speed

- Abrasive mass flow rate
- Abrasive type
- Viscosity

Work Piece based

- Workpiece Type
- Thickness
- Workpiece material properties
- Feed rate

The output parameters on which the machining is evaluated are:

- Depth of cut.
- Cutting forces,
- Rate of material removal.
- Surface finish.
- Kerf geometry.
- Nozzle wear.

3.12. LASER BEAM MACHINING

Laser means "**L**ight **A**mplification by **S**timulated **E**mission of **R**adiation". Laser Beam Machining (LBM) is a machining technique that employs a laser beam to process both metallic and non-metallic materials. In this method, a high-energy laser beam is directed onto the workpiece, transferring thermal energy to its surface. The intense heat generated causes the material on the surface to heat up, melt, and eventually vaporize, resulting in material removal from the workpiece.

3.12.1 Principle

Laser Beam Machining operates by focusing a high-energy laser beam onto the workpiece's surface. The energy from the laser is absorbed by the material, resulting in intense heating that causes the material to melt and vaporize. This mechanism facilitates the removal of material and allows for precise machining as shown in Fig. 3.21.

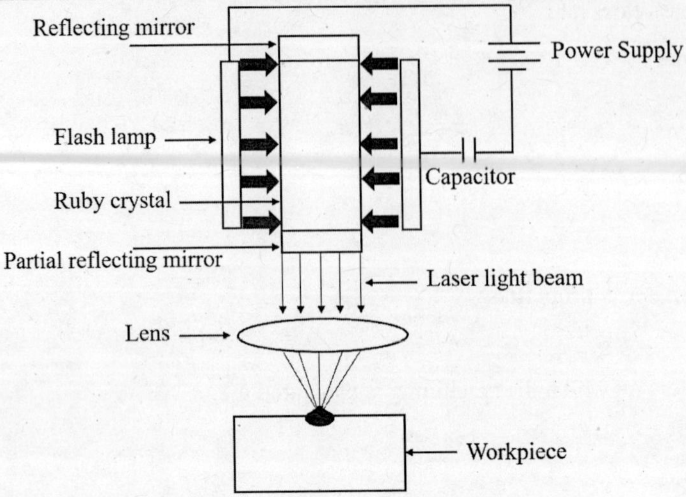

Fig. 3.21 Schematic of Laser beam machining

1. **Pumping medium:** A medium is needed that contains a large number of atoms. The atoms of the media are used to produce lasers.
2. **Flash Tube/Flash Lamp:** The flash tube or flash lamp supplies the energy required to excite the electrons in the atoms.
3. **Power Supply:** To produce light in flash lamp a power source of very high voltage is required.
4. **Capacitor:** Utilizing a capacitor is essential for operating the laser beam machine efficiently in pulse mode
5. **Reflecting Mirror:** Two types of mirrors are utilized: one is fully reflective, and the other is partially reflective. The fully reflective mirror is positioned at one end, while the partially reflective mirror is placed at the opposite end. The laser beam emerges from the side with the partially reflective mirror.

3.12.2 Working

Laser Beam Machining involves generating a high-energy laser beam, which is then focused onto the surface of the workpiece. Upon contact, the thermal energy from the laser is transferred to the workpiece, causing the material to heat up, melt, and vaporize. This results in the removal of material from the workpiece, enabling the machining process.

Advantages:

- Non-contact process, minimizing tool wear.
- High precision and accuracy.
- Can machine hard and brittle materials.
- Suitable for complex geometries and intricate designs.
- Minimal heat-affected zone (HAZ) when properly controlled.

Disadvantages:

- High initial cost of equipment.
- Limited material thickness for machining.
- Requires skilled operators.
- Generation of toxic fumes during machining of certain materials.

Applications:

- Cutting: Metals, ceramics, plastics, and composite materials.
- Drilling: Fine holes in aerospace components and medical devices.
- Engraving: Permanent markings on surfaces such as logos or barcodes.
- Micromachining: Manufacturing microelectronics and precision components.
- In the medical field, hair removal and cosmetic surgery are performed.

3.13 ELECTROCHEMICAL MACHINING

Electrochemical Machining (ECM) is an advanced machining process that removes material from a workpiece through controlled anodic dissolution, based on the principles of electrochemistry. It is widely used for machining hard and complex materials, such as superalloys, which are difficult to machine with conventional methods.

3.13.1 Principle

ECM is based on Faraday's laws of electrolysis, where metal ions are dissolved from the workpiece (anode) into an electrolyte under the influence of an electric field. The cathode (tool) does not wear out because no significant material is removed from it during the process.

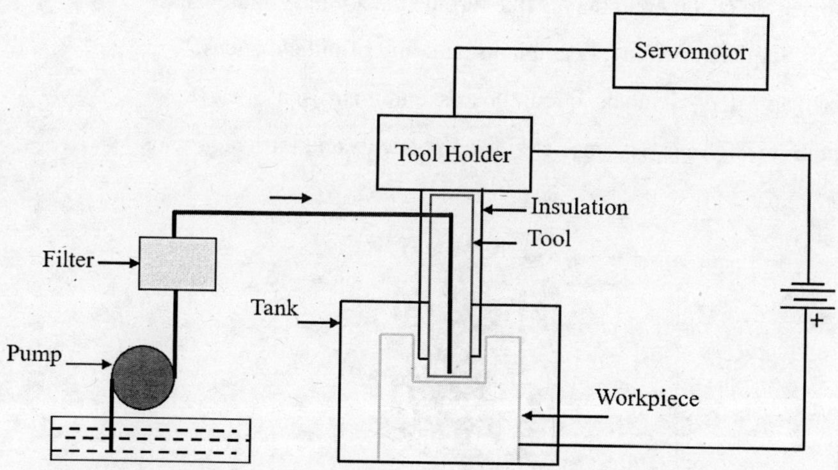

Fig. 3.22 Schematic of ECM

3.13.2 Construction of ECM

The construction of ECM is shown in Figure 3.22; it consists of the following components.

Power Supply:

- A DC power source is connected to the workpiece (positive, anode) and the tool (negative, cathode).

Tool (Cathode):

- Made of conductive material like copper or brass.
- Shaped to match the desired profile of the workpiece.

Workpiece (Anode):

- Must be electrically conductive.
- Made of metals like steel, titanium, or superalloys.

Electrolyte System:

- A pump circulates the electrolyte (e.g., NaCl or $NaNO_3$ solution) through the gap between the tool and the workpiece.
- The electrolyte removes dissolved material and prevents electrical contact.

Electrolyte Flow System:

- Ensures proper flow of the electrolyte to flush away dissolved material and maintain the machining gap.

Controller and Insulation:

- The machining process is controlled to ensure a precise material removal rate.
- The tool is insulated except for the machining area to ensure localized machining

3.13.3. APPLICATION OF ECM

- **Aerospace:** Precision components like turbine blades and engine parts.
- **Medical:** Surgical instruments, implants, and microfluidic devices.
- **Electronics:** Micro-channels, circuit boards, and micro-sensors.
- **Automotive:** High-performance engine components and intricate molds.

KNOW MORE

Modern Machining Processes

SUMMARY

This chapter was focused on non-traditional machining methods that offer advantages over traditional machining, such as handling complex shapes, harder materials, and precise micro-machining. Ultrasonic Machining (USM) uses high-frequency vibrations and abrasive slurry to remove material, ideal for brittle materials like glass and ceramics. Electric Discharge Machining (EDM) removes material via electrical sparks between the tool (electrode) and the workpiece in a dielectric fluid, with applications in intricate die and mold manufacturing. Wire Cut EDM uses a thin, continuously fed wire as the electrode to achieve precise cuts, suitable for complex contours. Abrasive Jet Machining (AJM) employs high-velocity abrasive particles for material removal, commonly used for delicate and heat-sensitive parts. Laser Beam Machining (LBM) utilizes a focused laser to vaporize material, ideal for precise and small-scale machining. Electrochemical Machining (ECM) involves anodic dissolution using an electrolyte for high-precision machining of hard metals. These processes are widely applied in aerospace, automotive, and electronics industries for their precision and material versatility.

EXERCISE

1. What is meant by conventional machining processes?
2. What is meant by Unconventional machining processes?
3. Explain the need for the development of the Unconventional Machining Process by considering any four simple cases of your own interest.
4. Differentiate the conventional and unconventional machining processes in terms of principles. (or) Distinguish between traditional and non-traditional machining processes.
5. What is the necessity for unconventional machining processes? (or) What is the importance of unconventional machining? (or) Enlist the requirement that demands the use of an advanced machining process.
6. Identify the mechanism of material removal, transfer media, and energy source for EDM, ECM, LBM, USM, and WEDM.
7. Explain the Principle, construction, and working of USM, and EDM process.
8. Discuss the input process parameter of the EDM.
9. Explain the output characteristics of the EDM machining process.
10. Explain in detail the abrasive water jet machining process.
11. State the advantages and limitations of USM.
12. What are the functions of dielectric fluid used in EDM?
13. What are the basic requirements of dielectric fluid used in EDM?
14. Explain the construction and working of an ECM process

15. Mention the best suited Unconventional machining process for the following operations:

- For producing microholes
- For machining small holes
- For machining deep holes
- For producing shallow holes
- For precision through cavities in workpieces.

REFERENCES

1. Ghosh, A. and Mallick, A.K. Manufacturing Science, 2nd edition, East-West Press (India) Pvt Ltd, 2010.
2. Goetsch, D.L., Advanced manufacturing technology, Delmar Publisher, (1990).
3. Jain, V.K. Advanced manufacturing process, (2009).

UNIT 4

CNC MILLING MACHINES AND MACHINE TOOL AUTOMATION

UNIT SPECIFICS

This chapter discusses the following topics:

- Introduction to machine centers and machine tool automation
- Explore the various types of control systems, automatic tool changers and tool magazine
- Discussion on G-codes and M-codes for programming
- Explore machine tool automation, using various tools
- Exploring the servo control system and Programming logic control (PLC)

CNC (Computer Numerical Control) milling machines are advanced machining tools used for precision cutting, drilling, and shaping of materials such as metal, plastic, and composites. Unlike conventional milling machines, CNC milling operates through computer-programmed instructions (G-code and M-code), ensuring high accuracy, repeatability, and efficiency in manufacturing. Automatic tool changers and high-speed spindles allow complex and intricate machining operations with minimal human intervention.

Machine tool automation refers to the integration of automated systems, to enhance the efficiency, precision, and productivity of machine tools. Automation in machining includes different control units. Further, this chapter briefly gives an introduction to programming logic control (PLC).

RATIONALE

The integration of CNC milling machines and machine tool automation is essential for enhancing precision, efficiency, and productivity in modern manufacturing. These machines ensure high dimensional accuracy and repeatability, reducing human errors and enabling micron-level tolerances critical for industries such as aerospace, automotive, and medical devices. Automation minimizes downtime by allowing continuous, unattended operations, optimizing material removal rates, and reducing cycle times. Additionally, CNC machines offer flexibility in handling complex geometries and diverse materials, enabling fast prototyping and small-batch production. Cost efficiency is another key advantage, as automated tool paths optimize material usage, lower scrap rates, and reduce labor costs, contributing to sustainable manufacturing. Moreover, automation enhances workplace safety by minimizing direct human interaction with hazardous machine components and improving ergonomics. In conclusion, this unit is a strategic move towards achieving higher quality, cost efficiency, and sustainability in the rapidly evolving manufacturing landscape.

The integration of CNC milling machines and machine tool automation is essential for enhancing precision, efficiency, and productivity in modern manufacturing. These machines ensure high dimensional accuracy and repeatability, reducing human errors and enabling micron-level tolerances critical for industries such as aerospace, automotive, and medical devices. Automation minimizes downtime by allowing continuous, unattended operations, optimizing material removal rates, and reducing cycle times. Additionally, CNC machines offer flexibility in handling complex geometries and diverse materials, enabling fast prototyping and small-batch production. Cost efficiency is another key advantage, as automated tool paths optimize material usage, lower scrap rates, and reduce labor costs, contributing to sustainable manufacturing. Moreover, automation enhances workplace safety by minimizing direct human interaction with hazardous machine components and improving ergonomics. In conclusion, this unit is a strategic move towards achieving higher quality, cost efficiency, and sustainability in the rapidly evolving manufacturing landscape.

PRE-REQUISITES

Basics of production engineering and automation

UNIT OUTCOMES

The list of outcomes of this unit is as follows:

U4-O1: Explain the types of machining centers.

U4-O2: Construct CNC program using G-code and M-code.

U4-O3: Describe the single spindle automates and transfer lines.

U4-O4: Explain the control system elements for automated machines.

Unit-4 Outcomes	Expected Mapping with Course Outcomes (*1- Weak Correlation; 2- Medium correlation; 3- Strong Correlation*)					
	CO-1	**CO-2**	**CO-3**	**CO-4**	**CO-5**	**CO-6**
U4-O1	3	3	3	1	3	3
U4-O2	3	3	2	1	3	3
U4-O3	3	3	3	1	2	2
U4-O4	3	2	3	1	3	3

4.1 Introduction

This chapter explores vertical and horizontal machining centers (VMCs and HMCs), highlighting their precision, automation features like ATCs and CNC programming (G-codes and M-codes), and the integration of computer-aided part programming for efficiency. It also covers machine tool automation, including single spindle automates, transfer lines, control elements like limit and proximity switches, feedback systems, and the pivotal role of Programmable Logic Controllers (PLCs) in modern manufacturing.

- Traditionally, operations like turning, boring, drilling, milling, reaming and threading would be performed by moving the part from one machine tool to another until all machining is completed.
- The workpiece like a cylinder block of a compressor, moves from one machine to the next with one particular machining operation performed at each machine.
- The part is then transferred to another machine for another operation, and so on.
- One method of performing multiple operation on large number of work piece is to use transfer lines.
- The transfer line has multiple machine tools organised in a sequential arrangement.
- The workpiece automatically moves form one machine tool to the next till all the operation are completed
- Transfer lines are high volume production set ups but lack flexibility
- There are situations and products where transfer lines are not feasible, particularly when types of products to be machined vary rapidly
- A solution for this problem is machining and turning centres.
- A machining centre is computer-controlled machine tool capable of performing a variety of cutting operations on different surfaces of a workpiece without having to move the workpiece from one machine to another.
- These machines have flexibility and versatility that other machines lack. They have thus become popular for mass production of jobs involving a variety of operations on different surfaces.
- The workpiece on a machining center is placed on a pallet or module that can be moved in different directions and can be rotated about one or more axes on the pallet.
- After a particular cutting operation has been completed, the workpiece is not required to move to another machine. In other words, the tools and machines are brought near the workpiece.
- The machining center is equipped with a programmable automatic tool changer. Depending on the operation to be performed, up to 200 cutting tools can be stored on the magazine.
- The cutting tools are automatically indexed with random access. The tool exchange arm swings around to pick up a particular too and place it in the spindle
- Tools are identified with coded tags, bar codes, or memory chips attached to the tool holder. Tool changing time typically ranges between 5 to 10 seconds.
- Touch probes are used for determining workpiece and tool position and surfaces relative to the machine table or column
- Once all cutting operations are finished, the pallet carrying the completed workpiece is automatically moved away, and a new pallet with a fresh workpiece is brought into position by an automatic pallet changer.

4.2 Classification of machining centers

Machining centers are generally classified into two types:

1. Vertical spindle machining center
2. Horizontal spindle machining centre

4.2.1 Vertical spindle machining center

Vertical machining centers are machines suitable for performing various machining operations on a flat surface with deep cavities. They are used for making moulds and dies. The machines are quite similar to vertical spindle milling machines but are computer-controlled and provided with an automatic tool changer (ATC), automatic pallet changer (APC), and tool magazine facilities. Figure 4.1 shows the schematic of the simple vertical machining center. The machining center is provided with five axes of movement shown in the figure to facilitate machining operations on all sides of the workpiece. These motions are shown in Table 1:

Table 4.1 Movement of axes

X and Y	Linear motions of the work table
Z	Linear motion of spindle head
R	The rotary motion of work table
S	Tilting motion of spindle head
T	Motion of ATC arm

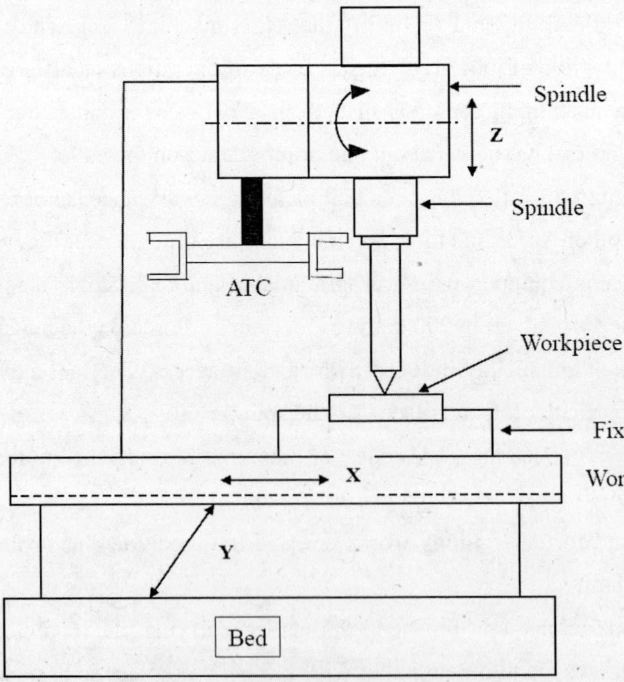

Fig. 4.1 Vertical machining center

4.2.2 Horizontal Machining Center

This machining centre is designed for handling large and tall workpieces that demand machining across multiple surfaces. The pallet is capable of being swivelled around various axes, allowing for machining at multiple angular positions. Chips drop out of the way during machining, providing an uncluttered view of the cut and preventing the recutting of chips. The table indexing capability enables multiple sides of a workpiece to be machined in one setup. Easy to provide automatic pallet changing (APC) (Figure 4.2).

The disadvantages of the horizontal machining center are:

- Heavy tools deflect.
- Fixtures must absorb the trust in the cutting tools.
- It is generally more expensive than the vertical spindle machine.

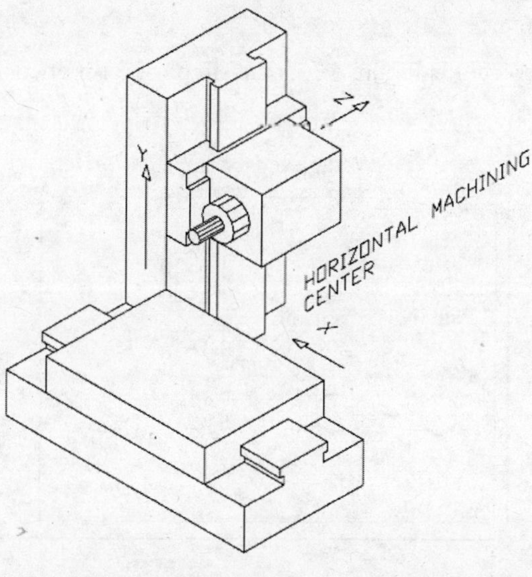

Fig. 4.2 Horizontal Machining Centre (Bohez., 2002)

4.3 Automatic tool changer and magazine

An automatic tool changer (ATC) is a device commonly used in manufacturing processes, particularly in machining, woodworking, and metalworking industries. Its primary function is automatically changing tools on a machine, such as a CNC (Computer Numerical Control) machine, without requiring manual intervention. The purpose of the automatic tool changer is to swap out the cutting tool with a new one for the upcoming machining task.

4.4 Tool magazine

The ATC is often accompanied by a tool magazine, which is a storage unit that holds various tools required for machining or manufacturing operations. These tools can include drills, end mills, taps, reamers, and other cutting or shaping implements.

The choice of the cutting tool from the magazine can be either random or sequential. Random tool selection offers greater flexibility than sequential methods, making it a popular choice among users. Every tool in the system has a unique identification mark and is stored in a designated pocket in the magazine. When a tool needs to be changed, the changer arm removes the previous tool and places it back in its designated pocket. A changer arm follows the instructions from a programmed tape, fetches the next tool from the magazine, and replaces it with the previous tool.

In sequential tooling, the tools are loaded in the rotary tool magazine in the precise order they will be used for machining, ensuring a smooth and efficient process. Failure to follow the correct loading order for the tools can result in the use of the wrong tool and the subsequent execution of the wrong operation.

4.5 Control System Machine Tool System

4.5.1 Point-to-point system

Point-to-point control, as depicted in Figure 4.3, is the simplest form of control systems.

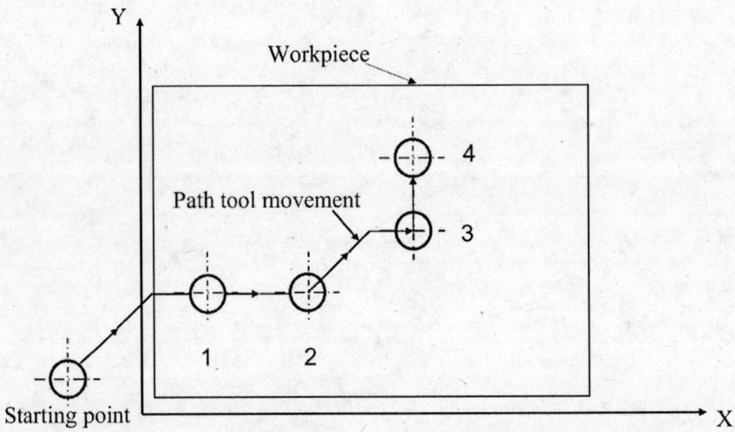

Fig. 4.3 Point-to-point based control system

In this system, the movement of the cutting tool between predefined positions is crucial, while the specific path taken by the tool is not significant. This control mode is commonly utilized in NC machines for operations such as drilling, punching, and spot welding, where tasks are performed at specific positions. It is also the most cost-effective mode among all control methods.

4.5.2 Straight cut system

This is an extension of a point-to-point control system by incorporating the capability for straight-line cutting or machining. The straight-line motion is achieved by regulating the tool's feed rate along a single-axis direction at a time, as illustrated in Figure 4.4. Typical applications of this control mode include operations such as face milling, pocket milling, and stepped turning.

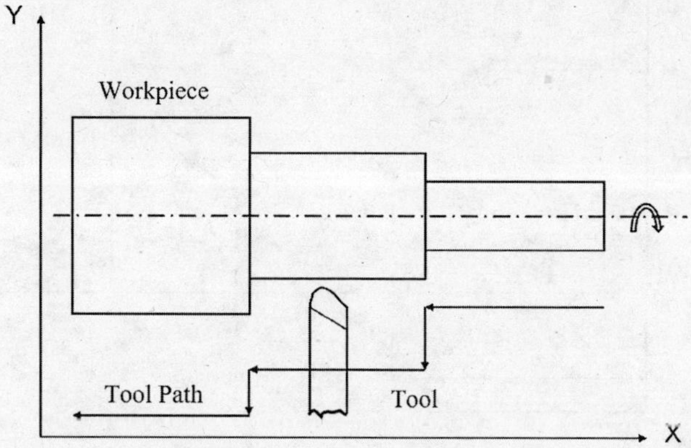

Fig. 4.4 Straight-cut system

4.5.3 Contouring path control system

The contouring path control system illustrated in Figure 4.5 facilitates continuous, simultaneous, and coordinated movements of the cutting tool and workpiece across multiple axes. Such control enables the machining of different contoured profiles and curved surfaces. In this control mode, most of the slide motions are controlled simultaneously so that their relative positions pass through the desired contoured path of the final shape of the required product.

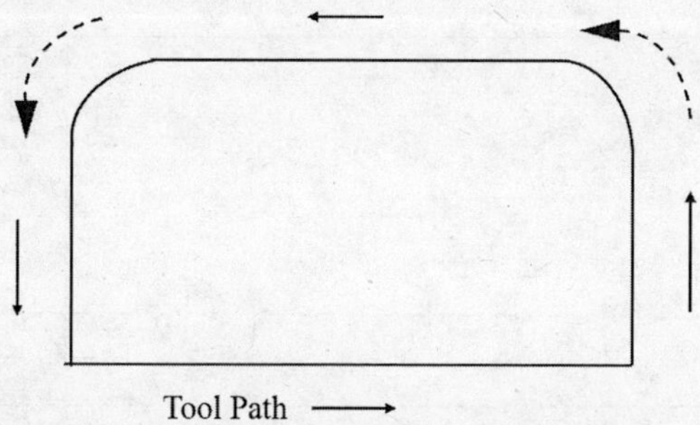

Fig. 4.5 Contouring path control system

4.6 According to programming methods

While machining certain components, it is necessary to specify the path for tool movement. Therefore, the geometric data of the component is converted into a machine-understandable program. This geometric data can be expressed in two ways:

1. Absolute programming system
2. Incremental programming systems

4.6.1 Absolute Programming Systems

In a cartesian coordinate system using absolute measurement, each point is specified using same zero established for a given coordinates system, as shown in Figure 4.6.

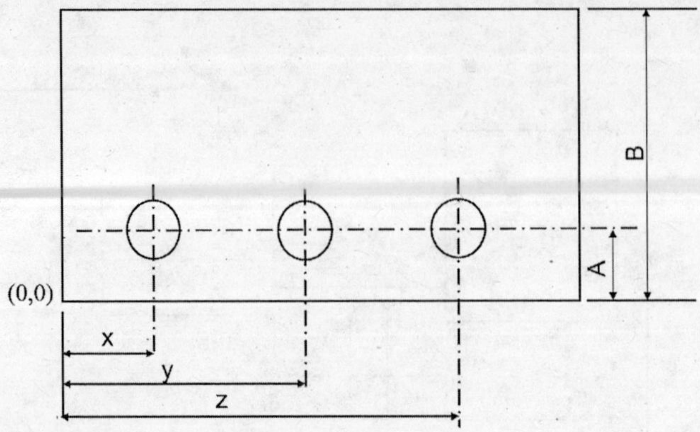

Fig. 4.6 Absolute system

In this case, the reference point (Zero) is the left-hand bottom corner of the workpiece and all the dimension are given from the point. A drawback of this system is that if an error creeps in a dimension, it continues to be so in that particular dimension.

4.6.2 Incremental Programming systems

In cartesian coordinates geometry system using incremental measurement, each point is specified using the path differential from the proceeding point position. So, in such programming, controller must store and process incremental path measurement, as shown in Figure 4.7.

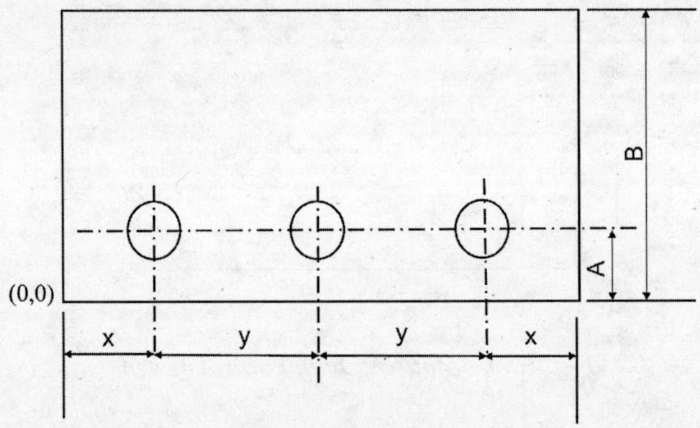

Fig. 4.7 Incremental system

4.7 According to type of controller

According to type of controller used, the machine tool systems are divided into two types:

1. Numeric control (NC) based controller
2. Computer numeric control (CNC) based controller

4.7.1 NC based controller systems

The NC controller was developed keeping in mind the control hardware available during the 1960's. The NC controllers employ voltage pulses to control various motions of the digital controller. These pulses can be actuated by a stepper motor or servo motor. The number of pulses to each axis is equivalent to the required incremental motion in that respective motor. These are pure command-based control and feedback systems, as shown in Fig 4.8.

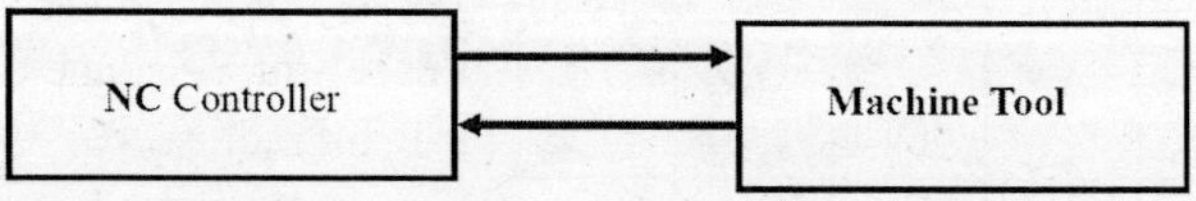

Fig. 4.8 NC-based controller system

4.7.2 CNC based controller system

The CNC controllers were developed during 1970s and employ a computer to control various motion of machine tool actuators through digital control. Such system eliminates the need of additional hardware system, required for hardware-based NC system, and hence CNC controller are mostly software based, which are more flexible and adaptable as per the changing need of customer requirement. The components of CNC controller as shown in Fig 4.9.

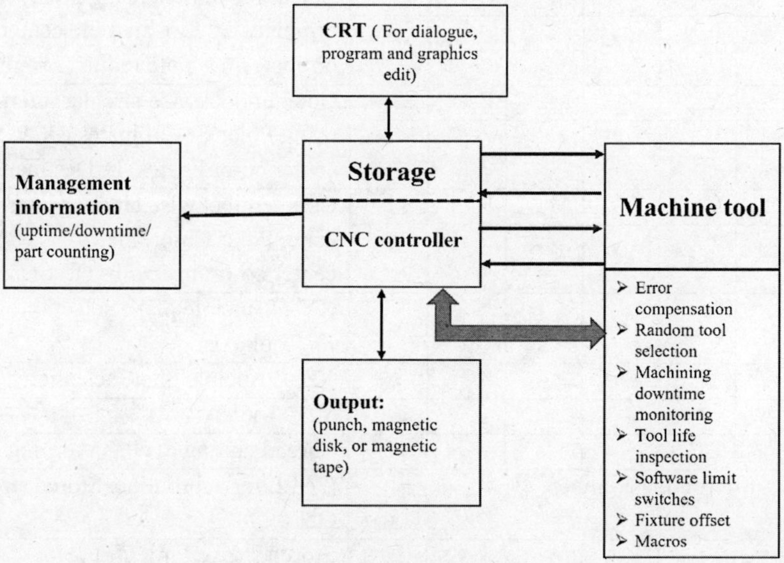

Fig. 4.9 CNC controller

4.8 Common preparatory function (G- codes)

The different preparatory functions (G codes) used in part programming are given in Table 2. These codes may vary depending on the controller.

Table 4.2 G- codes

G-code	Required axis/ other inputs						Function
G00	X	Y	Z	M	F	S	Rapid point-to-point positioning, rapid travel–axis motion at maximum speed
G01	X	Y	Z	M	F	S	Linear interpolation straight linear axis motion at a controlled feed rate

G-code	Required axis/ other inputs						Function
G02	X	Y	Z	M	F	S	Clockwise circular interpolation (Two axis in singe program block). "I & J" for XY plane "J & K" for YZ plane "I & K" for YZ plane Or R for radius
	I	J	K	R			
G03	X	Y	Z	M	X	Y	Counterclockwise circular interpolation or R= radius
	I	J	K	R			
G04	I						A dwell, stoppage of axis motion, for a programmed length of time, I = Delay in seconds
G10	X	Y		M	F	S	Tool length offset value, Rapid movement using polar Co-ordinates X & Y are pole center co-ordinates, I = pole radius, J = pole angle
	I	J					
G11	X	Y		M	F	S	Linear movement using polar Co-ordinates, X & Y are pole center co-ordinates, I = pole radius, J = pole angle
	I	J					
G12	X	Y		M	F	S	Counterclockwise circular interpolation using Polar Co-ordinates, X & Y are pole center co-ordinates, I= Destination angle
	I						
G13	X	Y		M	F	S	Counterclockwise circular interpolation using Polar Co-ordinates, X & Y are pole center co-ordinates, I= Destination angle
	I						
G17							XY= Principle plane selection Z= Tool axis
G18							XZ= Principle plane selection
G19							YZ= Tool axis
G21							Thread cutting cycle on turning centres
G22	C = Subroutine Number						CALL for subroutine, Stored stroke limit ON
G23							Stored stroke limit OFF
G24							Endface turning cycle
G25							Do loop
G27	U	V	W				Zero reference point return check
G28	U	V	W				Zero return or home position of tool
G code	**Required axis/ other inputs**						**Functions**
G29	U	V	W				Return from reference point
G30	U	V	W				Return to second reference point
G31							Skip cutting
G32	X	Y	Z	M	F	S	Clockwise helical interpolation K = pitch
	I	J	K				
G33	X	Y	Z	M	F	S	Thread cutting, constant lead or counter-clockwise, Clockwise helical interpolation
	I	J	K				

G-code	Required axis/ other inputs						Function
							K = pitch
G34							Thread cutting, increasing lead
G35							Thread cutting, decreasing lead
G37	B = Programming label no.						Programme label
G40							CANCEL, cutter radius compensation in milling or tool nose radius in lathes, or cutter compensation OFF
G41							cutter radius, tool nose radius compensation or Offset, left
G42							cutter radius, tool nose radius compensation or offset, Right
G43							Tool length compensation (positive)
G44							Tool length compensation (Negative)
G49							Tool length compensation OFF
G50	X	Y	Z				Axis preset command in lathe, position redefining
G53	X	Y	Z				Scaling- X, Y, Z define scale, Center, I, J, & K are scale factors
	I	J	K				
G54							Cancel scaling
G55	X	Y					Mirror about X-axis: X 0.0 Y1.0, About Y axis: X 1.0 Y 0.0, About X & Y axis: X 1.0 Y 1.0
G56							Cancel Mirror
G60	X	Y	Z	M			Pitch error compensation table
	I	J	K				
G61							Pitch error compensation ON
G62							Pitch error compensation OFF
G63							Tapping mode
G64							Cutting mode
G65							Macro calling
G66							Macro model call
G67							Macro model call CANCEL
G68							Mirror image for double turret ON
G69							Mirror image for double turret OFF
G70							Inch mode programming
G71							Metric mode programming
G72	X	Y	Z	M	F	S	Corner chamfer cycle, or finishing cycle for turning centers
	I	J	K				
G73	X	Y	Z	M	F	S	Corner radius cycle, rough face & rough turn cycle
	I	J	K				
G74	X	Y	Z		F	S	Stock removal in facing on turning centers, D = Depth of cut
	I	J	K			D	
G75	X	Y	Z	M	F	S	Pattern repeating
	I		K				

G-code	Required axis/ other inputs						Function
G76	X	Y	Z	M	F	S	Boring in turning centers
	I		K				
G77	X		Z	M	F	S	Grooving on X-axis
	I		K				
G78	X		Z	M	F	S	Multiple threading cycle
	I		K				
G80							CANCEL Canned cycle
G81	X	Y	Z	M	F	S	Basic drilling cycle
G82	X	Y	Z	M	F	S	Counter-boring cycle, I = Delay in seconds
	I						
G83	X	Y	Z	M	F	S	Peck drilling cycle, I= Delay in second, K= Peck depth
	I		K				
G84							Tapping cycle
G85	X	Y	Z	M	F	S	Boring or reaming cycle
G86							Rapid boring
G87							Boring back
G88							Boring manual dwell
G89							Boring dwell
G90							Absolute programming (default)
G91							Incremental programming/ positioning
G92							Repositioning or resting origin point
G93						S	Range RPM., inverse feed rate
G94							Feed rate programming in mm/min
G95							Feed rate programming in mm/rev
G96							Constant surface speed control
G97							Constant surface speed control CANCEL
G98	C = Subroutine Label no						Subroutine label, Return to initial levels
G99							Return to reference level

4.9 Common Miscellaneous Function (M- codes)

The common miscellaneous codes (M-codes) used in part program are given in Table 3. These codes may vary depending on the controller.

Table 4.3 M – Codes

M-Code	Function
M00	Program STOP- terminate the auto operation
M01	Optional or planned stop
M02	Programme END
M03	Spindle ON- forward/clockwise rotation
M04	Spindle ON- forward/clockwise rotation
M05	Spindle OFF
M06	Tool change

M-Code	Function
M07	Coolant ON (flood)
M08	Coolant ON (mist)
M09	Coolant OFF
M10	Automatic clamp
M11	Automatic unclamp
M12	Synchronize multiple axes or tailstock quill OUT for lathe
M13	Spindle clockwise and coolant ON or tailstock quill IN for lathe
M14	Spindle counterclockwise and coolant ON
M15	Rapid motion – positive direction
M16	Rapid motion – negative direction
M17	Turret forward rotation, G/P out ON
M18	Turret reverse rotation, G/P out OFF
M19	Spindle orient and STOP
M30	END of tape-tape will rewind automatically; program REWIND
M31	Interlock bypass
M40	Low-speed range in geared lathes, dry run function ON
M41	Medium speed range in geared lathes, Dry run function OFF
M42	High-speed range in geared lathes
M47	Continuous program execution from start of the program
M48	Cancel M47
M49	Deactivate manual speed or feed override
M58	Cancel M59
M59	RPM hold
M98	CALL sub-program, END of pitch error compensation table
M99	Return to calling program, RETURN program sub-routine

4.10 Subroutine

Subprograms, also referred to as mini-programs or subroutines, are utilized when a specific part of a program needs to be repeated, such as in a boring cycle. These subprograms are stored at the end of the main program and can be called multiple times during its execution. Implementing subroutines helps reduce the overall program length and eliminates the need to repeat statements for machining features that are used multiple times.

4.11 Canned Cycle

The canned cycle in NC/CNC programs is also called the multiple-repetitive cycle. These cycles require a considerable amount of computer memory in order to be useful so that machine can be controlled properly. Some of the frequently used canned cycle is shown below in the regular programming format.

The steps in canned boring cycle are shown in Fig. 4.10.

N1	G85	U0.5	W1				Beginning of Boring Cycle
N2	G85	P10	Q10	U0	W0	F15	Boring Cycle with subprogram [P10,Q10] for calling finishing cycle whenever required with feed rate of 15 mm/min.

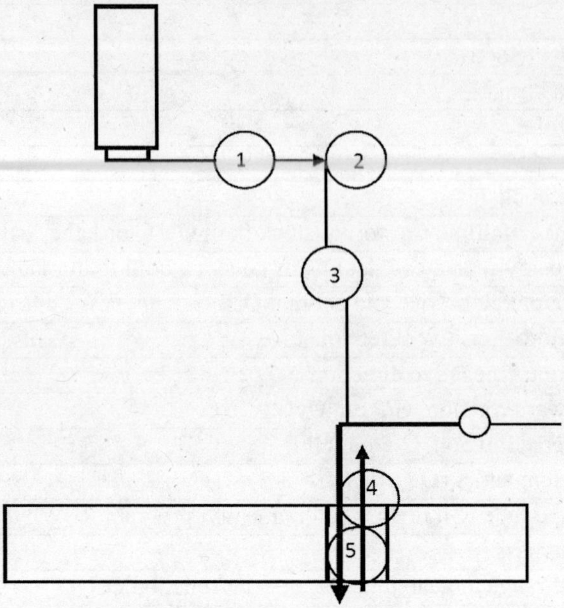

Fig. 4.10 Canned boring cycle

4.12 Principles of computer-aided part programming

Computer-Aided Part Programming (CAPP) is a process that involves the use of computer systems to the development of programs for manufacturing parts. These programs are used to control machine tools and equipment in a manufacturing environment. The principles of Computer-Aided Part Programming include:

Geometry Definition: Use CAD (Computer-Aided Design) software to define the geometric features of the part. This involves determining the shape, dimensions, and tolerances of the part.

Process Planning: Determine the manufacturing processes required to produce the part. This involves selecting the appropriate machining operations, such as milling, turning, drilling, etc.

Tool Selection: Select the appropriate tools for each machining operation. Factors to consider are the tool's shape, the type of material being worked with, and the specific cutting settings to be used.

Tool Path Generation: Generate the tool paths that the cutting tool will follow during machining. This involves determining the specific movements and coordinates of the tool to achieve the desired part geometry.

Simulation and Verification: Use simulation software to visualize and verify the machining process. This helps identify and rectify potential issues, such as collisions or inefficient tool paths before actual machining occurs.

Optimization: Optimize the machining process to improve efficiency, reduce cycle time, and minimize tool wear. This may involve adjusting cutting parameters, tool paths, or sequencing of operations.

Post-Processing: Generate the machine-specific code (G-code) that the CNC (Computer Numerical Control) machine understands. This code contains instructions for tool movements, speeds, and feeds.

Documentation: Create documentation for the machining process, including setup instructions, tool lists, and work instructions. This documentation helps ensure consistency and provides a reference for future production runs.

Integration with Manufacturing Systems: Integrate CAPP with other manufacturing systems, such as Enterprise Resource Planning (ERP) and Manufacturing Execution Systems (MES), to streamline the overall production process.

Feedback and Continuous Improvement: Collect feedback from the machining process and use it for continuous improvement. This may involve updating the part program based on performance data, implementing lessons learned, and refining the CAPP system.

By following these principles, Computer-Aided Part Programming aims to automate and optimize the process of creating machine instructions for the manufacturing of parts, ultimately improving efficiency, accuracy, and repeatability in production.

4.13. Machine tool automation

4.13.1. Introduction and need

The incorporation of automation into machine tools has significantly transformed production processes in contemporary manufacturing, resulting in improved efficiency, precision, and flexibility. The concept of machine tool automation pertains to the integration of automated systems and technologies into traditional machine tools, hence facilitating their ability to execute tasks with less human involvement. This introduction section focuses into the importance and necessity of machine tool automation within our modern industrial environment.

Need for tool automation:

a) **Enhanced productivity:** The implementation of automation in machine tools greatly enhances productivity by diminishing cycle durations, augmenting throughput, and facilitating uninterrupted operation. Automated systems have the capability to operate continuously without requiring intervals, resulting in increased total production rates.

b) **Improved precision and accuracy:** In comparison to human operation, automated machine tools exhibit enhanced precision and accuracy. The utilization of sophisticated control systems and sensors ensures the attainment of uniform and replicable machining procedures, hence yielding finished products of superior quality characterized by stringent tolerances.

c) **Cost efficiency:** Although the initial costs for automation systems may be greater, the long-term advantages in terms of decreased labour expenses, heightened output quantities, and reduced waste render automation a financially efficient alternative. Automation enhances the efficiency of resource allocation and reduces the cost of manufacturing per unit.

d) **Enhanced safety:** Automated processes effectively mitigate numerous safety risks that are commonly connected with human machining activities. Automation plays a crucial role in enhancing workplace safety and lessening the probability of accidents by diminishing the necessity for human involvement in tasks that have inherent risks, such as heavy lifting or exposure to moving machine components.

e) **Adaptability and flexibility:** The utilization of machine tool automation facilitates swift transitions and adjustments to satisfy diverse production demands and product criteria. Automated systems have the capability to seamlessly transition between various duties and part geometries, thereby enabling manufacturers to promptly adapt to evolving market demands.

f) **24/7 operation:** Automated machinery tools possess the capability to function in a continuous manner, encompassing periods of non-operational hours, weekends, and holidays. The capacity to produce at all times optimizes the use of equipment and guarantees prompt delivery of orders, consequently improving customer satisfaction and competitiveness.

g) **Data driven decision making:** Machine tool automation systems produce enormous quantities of real-time data pertaining to machine performance, production metrics, and quality indicators. By doing an analysis of this data, producers are able to find potential areas for process optimization, predictive

Machine tool automation is an essential component for modern manufacturing operations that aim to reach higher levels of productivity, quality, and competitiveness. Manufacturing companies may streamline their production processes, meet the ever-changing demands of the market, and maintain a competitive advantage in today's rapidly changing industrial landscape if they take advantage of the benefits that automation offers.

4.14 Single spindle automates

Single spindle automates, commonly referred to as single spindle automatic lathes, are specialized machine tools specifically designed to efficiently and accurately produce cylindrical components of small to medium sizes. These machines are essential in contemporary manufacturing, especially in industries that need large-scale production with strict precision requirements, such as automotive, aerospace, and electronics. A single spindle automates the process of using leverage to improve productivity, uniformity, and overall efficiency in manufacturing. Single spindle automates operate based on a fundamental idea where only one revolving spindle is utilized to grip and rotate the workpiece. Different cutting tools set up at different angles and feeds can do machine tasks like turning, drilling, threading, and knurling one after the other or all at the same time. The automation is accomplished by integrating mechanical, hydraulic, and electronic components that regulate the motion and functioning of both the spindle and cutting tools.

Key features and components: The machine is equipped with a single spindle, which serves as the main rotational axis for clamping the workpiece. This design enables meticulous manipulation of the workpiece's rotation and simplifies intricate machining procedures.

Tool Carriage: A carriage or turret is used to store and rotate various cutting tools. This feature facilitates rapid and effective tool replacements, allowing for a diverse array of machining tasks to be executed on the workpiece without the need for manual involvement.

Automatic bar feed: An automatic bar feed is a component commonly seen in single spindle automation systems. Its purpose is to supply the spindle with raw material. The continuous supply system is essential for efficient large-scale production since it minimizes interruptions and guarantees a steady flow of material.

CNC Control Systems: Contemporary single spindle automates are outfitted with CNC (Computer Numerical Control) systems that mechanize the regulation of machine operations. The CNC system accurately synchronizes the motions of the spindle and cutting tools, utilizing pre-programmed instructions, to guarantee precision and consistency.

Hydraulic and pneumatic systems: These systems are utilized to provide power for a range of machine operations, including tool changes, clamping, and feeding mechanisms. They offer the essential power and accuracy required for effective machine functioning.

Applications: Single spindle automates are extensively utilized in the manufacturing of small to medium-sized components, including:

- Automotive parts include shafts, pins, and bushings.
- Electronic components include connectors, housings, and screws.
- Aerospace components refer to fittings, fasteners, and minor structural parts used in the aerospace industry.

4.15 Transfer lines

Transfer lines are essential in machine tool automation since they significantly enhance efficiency and output. Transfer lines are production lines specifically engineered to facilitate the sequential movement of components or workpieces through different machining or assembly processes. These lines are commonly employed in high-volume production settings when there is a requirement to consistently and rapidly manufacture huge quantities of products.

A conventional transfer line is comprised of multiple workstations or machining centres, each fitted with specific tools or machinery to execute various operations on the workpiece. The aforementioned procedures encompass drilling, milling, turning, grinding, and other machining processes that are necessary for the production of the end component. A description of the operation of transfer lines is as follows:

a) **Loading station:** The first step is to load the transfer line with the raw materials or workpieces. The degree of automation in the factory determines whether personnel will manually load the containers or use automated loading equipment.

b) **Workstations:** In the process of their movement down the transfer line, the workpieces go through a number of distinct workstations, each of which is tasked with a particular machining or assembly activity. Every workstation is outfitted with a unique set of equipment or pieces of machinery that are specifically designed to carry out a particular task.

c) **Material handling systems:** Material handling systems, such as conveyors, robots, or transfer mechanisms, are commonly integrated into transfer lines to enable the efficient movement of workpieces across several workstations. These systems ensure the seamless and effective movement of components throughout the manufacturing process.

d) **Automation and control:** Most of the time, transfer lines are highly automated, and sophisticated control systems are used to monitor and regulate the entire manufacturing process. The performance of the machine, the wear on the tools, the quality of the parts, and the production throughput are all monitored by these systems to ensure that the operation is at its best.

e) **Quality control:** It is necessary to incorporate quality control techniques onto transfer lines in order to ensure that the components that are manufactured are according to the proper standards and specifications. It is possible that this will require the utilization of sensors, gauges, or inspection systems in order to validate the dimensions, tolerances, surface finish, and various other quality measures.

f) **Unloading station:** After all of the machining or assembly processes have been performed, the finished items are removed from the transfer line and loaded into the warehouse. Depending on the configuration of the manufacturing facility, this stage may entail either manual or automated unloading, just like the loading process did during the previous step.

Transfer lines provide numerous benefits in the automation of machine tools, which include:

- **High efficiency:** By facilitating uninterrupted production with minimal periods of idleness, transfer lines increase output and productivity.
- **Consistency:** Transfer lines work in a certain order, which makes sure that every part goes through the same set of steps. This makes sure that the quality and accuracy of the measurements are always the same.
- **Cost savings:** Transfer lines can help reduce manufacturing expenses and increase total profits by streamlining the production process and cutting down on the amount of work that needs to be done by hand.

- **Scalability:** Transfer lines can be easily scaled up or down to accommodate changes in production volume or product mix, making them highly adaptable to evolving manufacturing needs.

Transfer lines, in general, play an important part in the automation of modern machine tools because they make it possible to fabricate precision-engineered components in large quantities and with high efficiency across a wide variety of fields.

4.16 Elements of control system

Control systems are crucial in the context of machine tool automation since they are responsible for regulating the operation of a wide variety of machine tools and processes in order to accomplish the necessary performance goals. Real-time monitoring, analysis, and adjustment of the behaviour of the machine tools are all done by these control systems, which are made up of a number of components that collaborate with one another. When it comes to the automation of machine tools, the following are the most important components of a control system:

a) **Input devices:** In machine tool automation, the parameters or commands for the machining process are specified using input devices. Operators or programmers can input commands like tool routes, cutting settings, or workpiece specifications via these devices, which can be touchscreens, keyboards, or specialized interfaces.

b) **Sensors:** Sensors play a vital role in the automation of machine tools, since they offer valuable insights on multiple facets of the machining procedure, encompassing position, velocity, temperature, and tool wear. The machine tool automation industry commonly employs several types of sensors, such as encoders, proximity sensors, temperature sensors, and force/torque sensors. The utilization of these sensors facilitates the control system in the monitoring of machine tool performance and enables the implementation of requisite adjustments to enhance the efficiency of the machining process.

c) **Controller:** The controller serves as the primary element of the control system, carrying out the task of analysing input commands and sensor feedback in order to produce control signals for the machine tools. Within the context of machine tool automation, controllers encompass an array that spans from basic programmable logic controllers (PLCs) to advanced computer numerical control (CNC) systems or motion controllers. In order to accomplish desired machining outcomes, such as accuracy, surface finish, and production efficiency, the controller is responsible for interpreting input commands, executing control algorithms, and adjusting machine tool parameters.

d) **Actuators:** Actuators are technological apparatuses that transform control signals produced by the controller into actual motion or action within machine tools. Actuators play a crucial role in the automation of machine tools as they are tasked with regulating the motion of cutting tools, workpieces, and various components of the machine tool. Machine tool automation commonly employs several types of actuators, such as servo motors, hydraulic cylinders, pneumatic actuators, and linear actuators. These actuators provide accurate positioning, control of speed, and application of force/torque throughout the machining process.

e) **Machine tools:** Machine tools refer to the physical equipment employed for the execution of machining tasks, encompassing activities such as cutting, milling, drilling, and turning. The control system in machine tool automation engages with machine tools to govern their functioning through the use of input commands and sensor feedback. To obtain the required machining results, this interaction may need the management of spindle speed, tool feed rate, axis motions, coolant flow, and other parameters.

f) **Feedback loop:** In machine tool automation, the feedback loop is the procedure of employing sensors to continuously monitor the machining process' performance and modifying machine tool parameters in response to feedback. The control system is capable of identifying deviations from the expected machining outputs and implementing real-time corrective measures to ensure process stability, precision, and efficiency by comparing actual sensor data with the desired objectives.

g) **Communication interfaces:** Communication interfaces allow sensors, controllers, actuators, and external devices to communicate and share data with each other and with the rest of the control system. Different types of communication interfaces are used in machine tool automation. These can be digital, like Ethernet/IP, Modbus, or Profibus, or analog, like sensor feedback and control signal transfer. It is possible to monitor, program, and handle many machine tools in a manufacturing environment from one place due to these interfaces, which make it easy for different parts of the control system to work together.

Having been considered, the components of a machine tool automation control system cooperate to coordinate and maximize the performance of machine tools, ensuring accurate control, high productivity, and reliable machining quality across a range of manufacturing applications. Control systems are essential to the automation and effectiveness of modern machining processes because they include input devices, sensors, actuators, controllers, machine tools, feedback loops, and communication interfaces.

4.17 Limit switches

Limit switches play a crucial role in the automation of machine tools, serving the purpose of detecting the presence or absence of items or determining the location of machine components within a predetermined range. Those switches are of crucial significance in ensuring the secure and effective functioning of automated machinery, as they provide the control system with valuable information regarding the system's physical condition. The following is an extensive explanation of limit switches in the context of machine tool automation,

Functionality

a) **Detection:** Limit switches have been designed to ascertain either the existence or nonexistence of an object, the termination of motion, or a certain location of a moving part within a machine.

b) **Control:** Control devices function by transmitting signals to the control system, instructing it to initiate, stop, reverse direction, or perform additional activities in accordance with the identified position or condition.

Categories of limit switches

a) **Mechanical switches:** These switches activate the switch contacts when an object or machine component reaches a preset position using physical mechanisms like levers, rollers, or plungers.

b) **Inductive limit switches:** The use of electromagnetic induction is employed by inductive limit switches to detect metallic items that fall within their detecting range. They are well-suited for applications that require non-contact sensing.

c) **Photoelectric limit switches:** The presence or absence of things can be determined using photoelectric limit switches through the use of light beams. It is possible to put them in severe conditions and they are suitable for detecting things regardless of the material they are made of.

d) **Ultrasonic limit switches:** For the purpose of determining the distance between objects, ultrasonic limit switches make use of ultrasonic waves. Additionally, they are resistant to dust, dirt, and other environmental variables, making them an ideal method for sensing objects that are either clear or opaque.

e) **Proximity limit switches:** A number of different sensing methods, including capacitive, inductive, and magnetic field sensing, are used by proximity limit switches in order to identify the presence of particular items.

Installation and configuration

- For the purpose of identifying crucial positions or limitations, limit switches are often installed in certain locations within the machine tool or along the route of moving components.
- In order to ensure accurate detection and dependable operation, it is necessary to properly modify and configure limit switches. This may involve adjusting the sensitivity, establishing the actuation point, or configuring the switch characteristics in accordance with the needs of the application.

Application areas

- **End to end travel detection:** Limit switches are often used in order to acknowledge the termination of movement of machine components, such as tool carriages, slides, or rotary axes, with the purpose of averting excessive movement and ensuring precise positioning.

- **Home position detection:** During the initialization or homing procedures, they are employed to set the reference or home position of machine axes.
- **Safety interlocks:** Safety systems incorporate limit switches to prevent machine motions from continuing when objects or personnel approach dangerous areas.
- **Part presence detection:** They are used to make sure that parts or workpieces are present at different steps of the assembly or machining process so that mistakes are prevented and quality is maintained.

Advantages

- **Enhanced safety:** Limit switches contribute to the safe functioning of automated machinery by delivering accurate position data. This feedback helps prevent accidents or damage to equipment, which makes limit switches an important component.
- **Improves accuracy:** Limit switches provide for accurate positioning and control of machine components, which ultimately leads to improved precision and repeatability in machining operations.
- **Increased efficiency:** Limit switches streamline the operation of machine tools by automating position detection and control operations. This results in increased productivity and decreased downtime for the machine tools.

In brief, limit switches are integral elements within the field of machine tool automation, providing a crucial function in the identification of locations, regulation of machine motions, and facilitation of secure and effective functioning. Limit switches play a crucial role in establishing accurate control and automation in a wide range of manufacturing processes due to their different forms and uses.

4.18 Proximity switches

The presence or absence of things within their detecting range can be determined by proximity switches, which are crucial components in machine tool automation. These switches use their sensing range to determine whether or not the objects are there without the need for direct physical touch. Position sensing, part detection, and safety monitoring are just some of the many areas of machine tool automation that are significantly impacted by these switches through their essential function. The following is an in-depth description of proximity switches in relation to the automation of machine tools:

Functionality

a) The operation of proximity switches is based on the principle of detecting changes in electromagnetic fields or the reflection of electromagnetic radiation induced by the presence of items within their sensing range. This is accomplished by detecting the presence of nearby objects.

b) A change in the switch's output signal is caused whenever an object enters the sensing range of a proximity switch. This change serves as an indication that the object is present.

c) There are wide range of proximity switches available, including inductive, capacitive, magnetic, and ultrasonic switches. Each of these types of proximity switches is designed to accommodate a certain set of applications and environmental conditions.

Types of proximity switches

a) **Inductive proximity switches:** The electromagnetic induction technique is used by inductive proximity switches in order to identify metallic items that are within their sensing range. The detection of the presence of metal components, tooling, or machine components is a typical application for them in the field of machine tool automation.

b) **Capacitive proximity switches:** When items with various dielectric constants are present, capacitive proximity switches are able to detect variations in capacitance that are induced by the presence of these objects. Plastics, liquids, and powders are examples of non-metallic materials that can be detected using these instruments to a certain extent.

c) **Magnetic proximity switches:** Detecting the presence of ferrous objects within their detecting range is accomplished by magnetic proximity switches through the use of magnetic fields. They are frequently utilized in applications that call for the identification of metal items without the need for physical touch.

d) **Ultrasonic proximity switches:** Ultrasonic proximity switches are devices that can detect items within their sensing range by sending out ultrasonic waves and measuring the amount of time it takes for those waves to reflect back from the objects. It is possible to apply them in surroundings that are dusty, dirty, or harsh because they are effective at detecting objects regardless of the material they are made of.

Installation and configuration

- In order to detect key positions, limits, or the existence of a part, proximity switches are often positioned in particular locations within machine tools or along the route of moving components.
- Adjusting and configuring proximity switches in the correct manner is absolutely necessary in order to make sure accurate detection and reliable performance. It is possible that this will include adjusting the sensing range, sensitivity, and various other characteristics in accordance with the requirements of the application.

Application areas

a) **Position sensing:** During the process of machining, proximity switches can be used to detect the position of various machine components, including tool carriages, slides, and rotary axes. This is done in order to ensure accurate positioning and control operations.

b) **Part detection:** As part of the process of machining or assembly, they are utilized to identify the either the presence or absence of workpieces, tools, or fixtures at various phases of the process. This helps to prevent errors and ensures that the operation runs smoothly.

c) **Safety monitoring:** Safety systems incorporate proximity switches that monitor the placement of machine guards, doors, or other safety mechanisms, thereby mitigating the risk of dangerous machine movements in the event of compromised access.

Benefits

- **Improved reliability:** Proximity switches provide a non-contact sensing capability, so eliminating the necessity for mechanical contacts that may experience wear and tear or malfunction over time. This characteristic enhances the dependability and durability of the system.
- **Extensive uses:** Proximity switches offer a variety of options for detecting objects, materials, and ambient variables, rendering them highly adaptable for a multitude of machine tool automation applications.
- **Enhanced productivity:** Proximity switches play a crucial role in enhancing the operational efficiency of machine tools by offering precise and reliable detecting capabilities. This, in turn, results in increased productivity levels and diminished periods of inactivity.

Proximity switches are essential components in the automation of machine tools because they allow for a non-contact detection of objects, positions, and conditions within the environment in which the machine is being constructed. Because of the large variety of types they come in, the flexibility with which they may be installed, and their dependability, proximity switches play an essential part in assuring the safe, efficient, and accurate functioning of machine tools across a wide variety of manufacturing applications.

4.19 Servo Control System

Servo controls represent a series of electrical, mechanical, hydraulic, and pneumatic devices, employed for controlling the positions of slides of machine tools. The following two types of servo control systems are used:

- Open loop system
- Closed loop system

- **Open loop system**

  The schematic arrangement of the open loop system is shown in Figure 4.11. The open loop control system does not have a feedback mechanism. These are basically digital types. Open-loop machine tool controls provide motion control but lack a feedback mechanism to compare the output with the input, which is necessary for improved control and correction of the drive system.

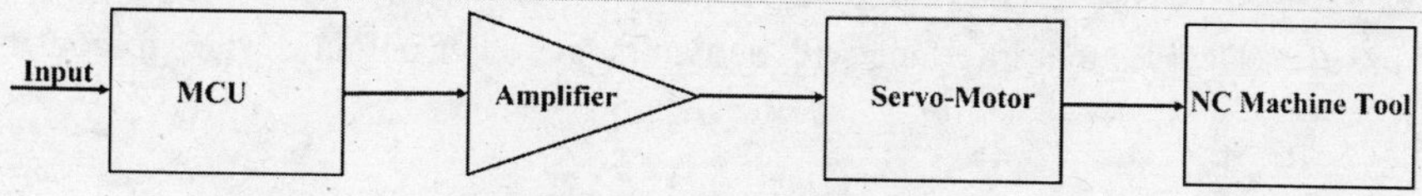

Fig. 4.11 Open loop system

- **Closed loop system**

A closed-loop control system includes a feedback mechanism. It features motion control with a feedback loop, enabling precise control of the drive system by continuously comparing the output with the input until the desired position is accurately achieved. In most of the cases, the feedback is measured by the monitoring devices to determine the drive displacement. The arrangement for the closed loop type of machine tool is shown in Figure 4.12.

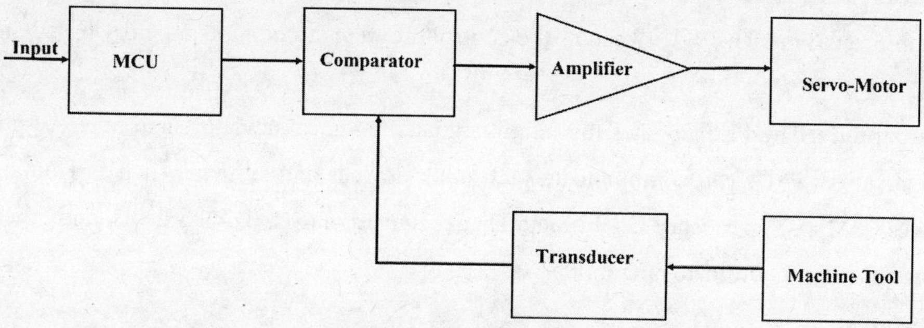

Fig. 4.12 Closed loop system

4.20 Programmable Logic Controller (PLC)

A Programmable Logic Controller (PLC) is a specialized digital computer designed for use in industrial automation and control systems. PLCs are designed to perform a wide range of control functions, from simple relay replacement to complex automation processes. They are extensively used in manufacturing plants, assembly lines, power plants, and various industrial applications where automation and control are crucial.

4.20.1 Introduction to PLCs

History: PLCs emerged in the late 1960s and early 1970s as a more flexible and reliable alternative to traditional relay-based control systems. They were initially developed to replace hard-wired relay systems used for industrial automation.

Component: A PLC consists of several components, including:

Central Processing Unit (CPU): It serves as the brain of the PLC, responsible for performing control tasks.

Input Modules: Devices that interface with sensors and other input devices to receive signals from the field.

Output Modules: Devices that interface with actuators and other output devices to control industrial processes.

Memory: Used to store the program logic, data, and system configuration.

Communication Ports: Allow the PLC to communicate with external devices and systems.

Programming: PLCs are programmed using specialized software, typically ladder logic programming language, which resembles electrical relay diagrams. Other programming languages like Function Block Diagram (FBD), Structured Text (ST), and Sequential Function Chart (SFC) are also supported by modern PLCs.

Operation: The functioning of a PLC follows following steps.:

Input Scan: The PLC reads input signals from input modules.

Program Execution: The PLC executes the control program stored in its memory based on the input signals.

Output Update: The PLC updates the output signals to control actuators and other output devices.

Communication: PLCs can communicate with other devices and systems, such as Human-Machine Interfaces (HMIs), Supervisory Control and Data Acquisition (SCADA) systems, and other PLCs, to exchange data and coordinate operations.

Applications:

PLCs are used in various industrial applications, including:

Manufacturing: Controlling assembly lines, robotic systems, and material handling processes.

Power Plants: Monitoring and controlling power generation, distribution, and equipment.

Automotive: Controlling manufacturing processes in automobile production lines.

Petrochemical: Managing processes in oil refineries, chemical plants, and pipelines.

Building Automation: Controlling HVAC systems, lighting, and security systems in commercial buildings.

Advantages:

PLCs offer several advantages over traditional relay-based control systems, including:

Flexibility: Easily reprogrammable for changes in process requirements.

Reliability: More reliable than relay-based systems due to solid-state components.

Compactness: Occupies less space compared to relay panels.

Diagnostics: Provides diagnostic features for troubleshooting and maintenance.

Integration: Easily integrates with other automation systems and devices.

4.21 Block Diagram of PLC

Figure 4.13 illustrates the block diagram of the programming logic controller (PLC). The basic components of the PLC are as follows:

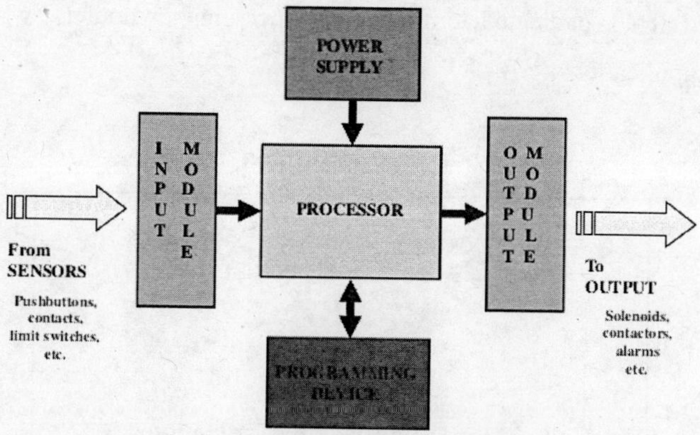

Fig. 4.13. Block diagram of PLC

Processor (CPU):

The processor section of a PLC is the central component that comprises of RAM, ROM, logic solver, and user memory. The central processing unit is the core component of a programmable logic controller. The CPU governs, monitors, and oversees all operations within the PLC. The central processing unit (CPU) processes and carries out control instructions by utilising the programme instruction stored in memory.

Input and Output Model:

The input module acts as a bridge between the input devices and the central processing unit (CPU), facilitating the conversion of analog signals into digital signals. The output module serves as an intermediary between output devices and the central processing unit (CPU), converting digital signals into analog signals.

Power Supply:

The power supply delivers electricity to the processor unit, as well as the input and output module units. It can be either an integrated component or a separately mounted unit. Most PLCs operate using 0 volts DC and 24 volts.

Memory:

Memory is used to store and retrieve data and information in PLC systems. Data memory is specifically utilized for storing numerical data needed for mathematical calculations, barcode information, and similar purposes. User memory, on the other hand, holds the application program created by the user.

Programming Devices:

Programming devices play a crucial role in PLC systems by allowing users to load programs into the program memory, edit them, and monitor their execution. Additionally, these devices are essential for troubleshooting ladder logic programs. Common examples of programming devices include handheld terminals (HHT), dedicated terminals, and personal computers, which are widely used across various PLC applications.

KNOW MORE

CNC Milling and Machine Tool automation

SUMMARY

This chapter discussed about the vertical and horizontal machining centers (VMCs and HMCs) are precision systems with distinct spindle orientations—VMCs for surface machining and HMCs for multi-sided operations. They feature axis identification (X, Y, Z, and rotational), electronic controls, automatic tool changers (ATCs), and tool magazines for automation. CNC programming uses G-codes (preparatory functions) and M-codes (miscellaneous functions) to execute machining tasks, including subroutines and canned cycles. Computer-aided part programming integrates design and manufacturing, enhancing precision and efficiency in machining processes.

Further, this Chapter included information about how machine tool automation enhances manufacturing efficiency and precision by reducing manual intervention. Single spindle automates and transfer lines are commonly used for high-volume production. Key components of automation include control system elements like limit switches and proximity switches for monitoring and control. Automation systems often employ feedback and servo control systems, represented in block diagrams, to ensure accuracy and responsiveness. Programmable Logic Controllers (PLCs), with their modular block diagrams, play a crucial role in automating and managing complex machining processes, making automation indispensable in modern manufacturing.

EXERCISE

1. What are the basic elements of numerical control systems
2. Explain point to point positioning control system and straight-cut positioning system
3. What is a machining center? Briefly describe the various types of machining centers.
4. What are the functions of an automatic tool changer? Give the advantages of using an ATC system.
5. Write a short note on G. codes and M. codes

6. Explain the following codes

   G01 G90 G97 MO3 MO6 To4

7. What are canned programs, and how are they used? Explain any one canned program.
8. Compare open-loop and closed-loop control systems.
9. Explain the difference between absolute programming systems and incremental programming systems.
10. Differentiate between machining centers and turning centers
11. Explain PLC with a block diagram
12. What are the different elements of control system

REFERENCES

1. https://machmotion.com/downloads/GCode/Mach4-G-and-M-Code-Reference-Manual.pdf
2. Production Technology – HMT, Banglore, Tata Mc-Graw Hill.
3. Raghuwanshi, B.S., Workshop Technology, Vol II, Dhanpat Rai and Co, (2015).

UNIT 5

SPECIAL PURPOSE MACHINES AND MAINTENANCE OF MACHINE TOOLS

UNIT SPECIFICS

This unit includes the following points:

- Discuss the concept of Special Purpose Machines (SPMs)
- Exploring the elements, improvement in productivity, and principles behind the SPMs
- Explaining the maintenance of the machine tool
- Discussion on the total productive maintenance

Special-purpose machines (SPMs) are custom-designed machines used for specific manufacturing tasks that cannot be efficiently performed by standard machines. Unlike general-purpose machines, SPMs are built to handle repetitive and high-volume production processes with greater precision, speed, and automation. The key advantages of SPMs include reduced cycle time, improved productivity, enhanced accuracy, and lower operational costs. On the other hand, maintenance of machine tools is essential to ensure the longevity, reliability, and efficiency of industrial equipment. Machine tools are subjected to wear and tear due to continuous operation, making proper maintenance practices crucial for preventing breakdowns and ensuring smooth production. Maintenance strategies can be categorized into preventive, predictive, corrective, and condition-based maintenance.

Both special-purpose machines and machine tool maintenance are integral to modern manufacturing. While SPMs enhance efficiency and precision in specialized production tasks, effective maintenance ensures machine tools remain operational, reducing downtime and improving overall productivity. Understanding these aspects is crucial for engineers and technicians to optimize industrial performance and maintain cost-effective production processes.

RATIONALE

The establishment of a special purpose machine (SPM) unit is a strategic investment aimed at enhancing manufacturing efficiency, precision, and automation in industries requiring high-volume and customized production. Unlike conventional machines, SPMs are designed to perform specific tasks with higher accuracy, speed, and cost-effectiveness, reducing reliance on manual intervention and minimizing production downtime. These machines are tailored to meet unique manufacturing requirements, ensuring higher productivity while maintaining quality standards. Additionally, SPMs contribute to sustainable manufacturing by minimizing energy consumption and reducing human error, leading to cost savings and improved output. Investing in a special-purpose machine unit not only enhances industrial competitiveness but also fosters innovation, customization, and long-term growth in modern manufacturing ecosystems.

The maintenance of machine tools is essential for ensuring the longevity, efficiency, and reliability of manufacturing operations across various industries. Regular maintenance minimizes downtime, reduces repair costs, and enhances the precision and performance of machine tools, which are critical for high-quality production. Investing in the maintenance of machine tools is crucial for achieving sustainable production, maintaining product quality, and enhancing the competitiveness of modern manufacturing enterprises.

PRE-REQUISITES

Basics of total quality control

UNIT OUTCOMES

The list of outcomes of this unit is as follows:

U5-O1: Describe principles and various elements of SPM.

U5-O2: Explain the different types of maintenance.

U5-O3: Explain the maintenance record.

U5-O4: Describe total productive maintenance (TPM) to ensure reliability and operational efficiency.

Unit-5 Outcomes	**Expected Mapping with Course Outcomes** (*1- Weak Correlation; 2- Medium correlation; 3- Strong Correlation*)					
	CO-1	**CO-2**	**CO-3**	**CO-4**	**CO-5**	**CO-6**
U5-O1	2	2	2	1	3	2
U5-O2	3	1	1	1	2	3
U5-O3	1	1	1	1	2	3
U5-O4	3	1	1	1	2	3

5.1 Introduction

This chapter covers Special Purpose Machines (SPMs), custom-designed for specific tasks to improve productivity, and highlights their efficient design principles. It also discusses machine tool maintenance, including preventive, predictive, and corrective approaches, supported by repair analysis, maintenance records, and Total Productive Maintenance (TPM) to ensure reliability and operational efficiency.

Precision and efficiency are the most important things in modern production and industrial automation. The importance of specialized equipment grows as industries change to meet the rising demand for high-quality goods and fast production rates. Special Purpose Machines (SPMs) are made to meet these exact requirements by providing custom solutions for jobs that regular machines aren't able to do well.

Special Purpose tools, or SPMs, are constructed tools that are made to do a certain job or set of tasks, usually in industrial or manufacturing settings. In contrast to general-purpose machines, which are designed to do multiple tasks, SPMs are specifically designed to do one task very quickly, accurately, and reliably. Whether they are being used for testing, putting things together, or processing materials, the job at hand determines how they are made and how they work.

5.2 General Element of SPM

1. **Frame and Structure:** The frame provides the basic structure and support for the machine. It is designed to withstand the forces and vibrations generated during the operation.
2. **Actuators:** Actuators are devices that provide controlled movement to different parts of the machine. Examples include hydraulic cylinders, pneumatic cylinders, and electric motors.
3. **Control System:** SPMs typically have a dedicated control system for managing the machine's operation. This can include PLCs (Programmable Logic Controllers), microcontrollers, or other specialized control units.
4. **Sensors:** Sensors are used to gather information about the workpiece, tool position, and other relevant parameters. Common types of sensors include proximity, optical, and pressure sensors.
5. **Tooling and Fixturing:** SPMs often include specialized tooling and fixtures designed for the specific manufacturing process. These ensure accurate positioning and secure holding of the workpiece during machining.
6. **Motion Control System:** This system controls the movement of various machine components with precision. It includes components like servo motors, stepper motors, and associated controllers.
7. **Power Transmission System:** The transmission system transfers power from the energy source to different machine components. This can include gears, belts, chains, and other mechanical components.
8. **Cooling and Lubrication Systems:** SPMs may incorporate systems for cooling and lubricating moving parts to prevent overheating and reduce friction.
9. **Human-Machine Interface (HMI):** An interface that allows operators to interact with and control the machine. It may include a touchscreen panel, buttons, and other input devices.
10. **Safety Features:** Special-purpose machines are equipped with safety features such as emergency stops, interlocks, and guards to ensure the safety of operators.
11. **Programming Interface:** For programmable SPMs, a programming interface allows the user to define and customize the machine's operation.

12. **Material Handling Systems:** Some SPMs may include automated material handling systems for loading and unloading workpieces.
13. **Quality Control Systems:** In some cases, SPMs may integrate quality control systems to inspect and verify the produced parts.

These elements work together to create a specialized machine tailored to a specific manufacturing process, providing efficiency, precision, and reliability. The design of Special Purpose Machines is highly application-specific, and each machine may have unique features based on the intended purpose.

5.3 Productivity Improvement by SPM

Productivity improvement by special-purpose machines involves the use of custom-designed equipment tailored to specific tasks within a production process. These machines are engineered to streamline operations, enhance efficiency, and ultimately boost productivity in manufacturing or industrial settings. Here's how they contribute to productivity improvement:

1. **Automation:** Special-purpose machines are designed to automate repetitive tasks that were previously performed manually or required multiple steps. By automating these tasks, productivity increases as machines can work continuously without fatigue or breaks.
2. **Speed and Accuracy:** These machines are optimized for speed and precision, performing tasks much faster and with higher accuracy than human labour. This reduces cycle times and minimizes errors, leading to overall productivity gains.
3. **Customization:** Special-purpose machines are tailored to specific manufacturing processes or operations. This customization ensures that the machine is optimized for the particular task it's designed to perform, leading to improved efficiency and productivity.
4. **Reduced Downtime:** Special-purpose machines are often engineered for reliability and durability. With fewer breakdowns and maintenance requirements compared to general-purpose machinery, downtime is reduced, allowing for more continuous production and higher overall productivity.
5. **Resource Optimization:** These machines are typically designed to use resources such as energy, materials, and space more efficiently. By optimizing resource utilization, special-purpose machines contribute to cost reduction and improved productivity.
6. **Process Integration:** Special-purpose machines can be integrated into existing production lines seamlessly. This integration optimizes workflows and eliminates bottlenecks, allowing for smoother operations and increased productivity across the entire manufacturing process.

5.4 Principles of SPM

Designing Special Purpose Machines (SPMs) involves adhering to specific principles to ensure the machine meets its intended purpose efficiently and effectively. While the design principles can vary based on the specific application, here are some general principles that are often followed in SPM design:

1. **Understand the Application Requirements**: Before starting the design process, a thorough understanding of the specific manufacturing process and its requirements is essential. This includes knowledge of tolerances, production rates, and other critical parameters.
2. **Customization for Specific Tasks:** SPMs are designed to perform a particular task or set of tasks with high precision and efficiency. The design should be tailored to meet the specific requirements of the intended application.
3. **Simplicity in Design:** Keeping the design simple helps in minimizing complexity, reducing costs, and enhancing reliability. Unnecessary features that do not contribute to the machine's primary function should be avoided.
4. **Modularity:** Designing SPMs with modular components allows for easier maintenance, repair, and future modifications. Modular designs also facilitate scalability if the production requirements change.
5. **Optimization of Material and Energy Usage:** Efficient use of materials and energy is crucial for cost-effectiveness. This involves selecting materials with the right properties and optimizing the machine's energy consumption.
6. **Precision and Accuracy:** SPMs are expected to deliver high precision and accuracy in manufacturing processes. The design should focus on minimizing errors, backlash, and other factors that could affect the quality of the end product.
7. **Reliability and Durability:** SPMs are often employed in industrial settings where reliability is paramount. Designs should prioritize robustness and durability to ensure continuous and trouble-free operation over an extended period.
8. **Ease of Operation and Maintenance:** The design should consider the ease of operation for machine operators and maintenance personnel. Intuitive interfaces, clear labelling, and easy access to critical components contribute to efficient operation and maintenance.
9. **Safety Considerations:** Safety is a top priority in SPM design. Adequate safety features, such as emergency stops, interlocks, and guards, should be integrated to protect operators and prevent accidents.
10. **Cost-Effectiveness:** SPM design should strike a balance between functionality and cost. The goal is to achieve the required performance at a lower cost, considering factors such as material costs, manufacturing processes, and the overall economic feasibility.
11. **Adaptability to Changes**: The design should allow for adaptation to changes in production requirements or technological advancements. Flexibility in design can future-proof the SPM to some extent.
12. **Environmental Considerations:** Where applicable, consider the environmental impact of the machine's operation. This includes energy efficiency, waste reduction, and adherence to environmental regulations.

13. **Testing and Validation:** Rigorous testing and validation processes should be implemented to ensure that the SPM meets design specifications and performs reliably under various conditions.

By adhering to these principles, designers can create Special Purpose Machines that effectively address the specific needs of a given manufacturing process while ensuring efficiency, reliability, and safety.

5.5. Maintenance of Machine Tools

Types of maintenance

In many different industries, machine tools are crucial because they make it possible to manufacture components and parts that are of a high level of precision. On the other hand, adequate maintenance is very necessary in order to guarantee optimal performance and longevity. Maintenance strategies for machine tools can be roughly classified into a number of different sorts, each of which serves a unique purpose and addresses a different component of machine maintenance. When it comes to machine tools, there are many forms of maintenance that can be performed, each of which involves analysing their qualities, advantages, and respective implementation strategies.

5.5.1 Preventive maintenance

Preventive maintenance is the practice of taking proactive steps to avoid equipment breakdown. This maintenance type focuses on detecting and resolving possible problems by doing routine inspections, lubrication, calibration, and replacing components. Following a predetermined maintenance schedule helps reduce machine downtime and prolong the equipment's lifespan. Preventive maintenance involves scheduled examinations and servicing.

- Scheduled inspections and servicing.
- Lubrication of moving parts.
- Adjusting machine parameters precisely.
- Replacing worn-out parts
- Implementation of condition monitoring techniques.

5.5.2 Condition based maintenance

Condition-based maintenance involves monitoring equipment condition continuously to decide when maintenance should be performed. By analysing real-time data and status indicators, maintenance actions may be scheduled as needed to optimize resource usage and reduce downtime. Essential elements of condition-based maintenance comprise:

- Supervising equipment settings and performance metrics.
- Maintenance operations triggered based on specific thresholds.
- The use of predictive analytics and machine learning integration.
- Adaptable maintenance schedule adjustments.
- Emphasize optimizing equipment uptime and reliability.

5.5.3 Predictive maintenance

Predictive maintenance uses data analysis and monitoring methods to anticipate when equipment failure is probable. Early detection of potential faults is possible through the collection and analysis of data from different sensors and monitoring systems, enabling prompt intervention and maintenance actions. Important components of predictive maintenance are:

- Continuous monitoring of machine performance.
- Conducting data analysis to detect changes and defects.
- Predictive modeling to estimate remaining usable life.
- Instant alerts and notifications in real-time.
- Combining sensors and IoT technologies.

5.5.4 Reactive maintenance

Reactive maintenance, sometimes referred to as breakdown or corrective maintenance, entails dealing with equipment faults as they arise. This method is used for non-essential equipment or when the expense of preventative actions is more than the advantages, notwithstanding the potential for more downtime and higher repair expenses. Reactive maintenance is characterized by responding to equipment failures as they occur.

- Responding to unexpected equipment malfunctions.
- Immediate repairs to reinstate functionality.
- Performing emergency troubleshooting and diagnostics.
- Inadequate planning and scheduling.

Implementing efficient maintenance techniques is crucial for ensuring the reliability, effectiveness, and durability of machine tools across different industrial settings. Organizations can create customized maintenance plans by comprehending several maintenance kinds such as preventive, predictive, reactive, and condition-based, aligning them with their specific needs and operational demands. Firms can boost productivity by implementing proactive maintenance practices and utilizing sophisticated technology to optimize equipment uptime and reduce maintenance expenses.

5.6 Repair cycle analysis

Repair Cycle Analysis in machine tools is a systematic approach used to examine and enhance the efficiency and efficacy of repairs carried out on machine tools after equipment breakdowns or failures. The analysis seeks to decrease downtime, lower maintenance expenses, and improve equipment reliability. Repair cycle analysis involves

- **Locating Breakdowns in Equipment:** The procedure begins by realizing and documenting occurrences of equipment failures or breakdowns. Possible issues may involve problems in different parts including motors, bearings, control systems, or structural elements of the machine tool.

- **Documentation of Repair Activities:** Each repair performed on the machine tool is meticulously documented. The information required includes the specific day and time of the failure, the type of failure, any parts or components that were replaced, the repair methods employed, and the length of time taken for the repair.
- **Downtime Analysis:** An analysis is conducted on the duration of downtime caused by equipment breakdowns. This involves keeping track of the duration from the moment of failure to the point when the machine tool was restored to full functionality. Downtime can be categorized according to its severity and influence on output.
- **Root Cause Analysis:** Root Cause Analysis is performed to identify the fundamental reasons for equipment malfunctions. This includes investigating problems such as mechanical breakdown, lack of proper servicing, insufficient operator training, low-quality components or materials, environmental factors, or design deficiencies.
- **Repair Time Analysis:** The amount of time required to finish each individual repair task is evaluated. The amount of time spent diagnosing the problem, placing orders for new parts, carrying out the repair, and performing post-repair testing and validation is included in this measurement.
- **Cost Analysis:** The costs related to repairs are evaluated, including both direct and indirect expenses. Direct costs encompass the expenditures for replacement parts, labour, and specialized repair services outsourced. Indirect costs may encompass losses from production halts, overtime pay, and effects on consumer satisfaction.
- **Identification of Improvement Opportunities:** Opportunities for enhancement are indicated based on the analysis results. Possible actions include optimizing repair procedures, introducing preventative maintenance strategies, strengthening maintenance staff training programs, improving spare parts inventory management, or updating equipment components to enhance reliability.
- **Implementation of Corrective Actions:** Action plans are created and put into effect to tackle the improvement possibilities that have been identified. Tasks may include adjusting maintenance schedules, acquiring sophisticated diagnostic tools, improving inventory management systems, or offering extra training to maintenance personnel.
- **Performance Monitoring:** The efficacy of the corrective measures is continually assessed. Key performance indicators (KPIs) like mean time between failures (MTBF), mean time to repair (MTTR), and overall equipment effectiveness (OEE) are monitored to evaluate the effects of enhancements on equipment dependability and operational efficiency.
- **Continuous Improvement:** Repair cycle analysis is a continual procedure focused on enhancing performance. Periodic evaluations and audits are carried out to pinpoint new difficulties and

chances for more optimization. To improve repair procedures and ensure long-term gains in machine tool performance and reliability, feedback from operators, maintenance staff, and other stakeholders is requested.

Organizations can optimize their manufacturing operations by analysing repair cycles methodically, making specific adjustments to minimize downtime, reduce repair costs, and enhance the overall dependability and efficiency of their machine tools.

5.7 Repair complexity

In the context of machine tools, "repair complexity" refers to the level of difficulty or intricacy in resolving difficulties or malfunctions within the equipment. This word refers to a range of factors that affect the difficulty of repairs, such as the problem's type, component accessibility, technical documentation availability, maintenance personnel's skill level, and resources needed for the repair.

- **Nature of the problem:** Frequently, the intricacy of a repair is determined by the particular characteristics of the issue that impacts the machine tool. Certain problems may be quite simple to identify and rectify, including minor adjustments or regular maintenance duties. Nevertheless, intricate issues, such as malfunctioning systems or component defects, might necessitate substantial efforts in troubleshooting and restoration.
- **Accessibility of Components:** The degree to which maintenance personnel are able to access the damaged components has a significant impact on the intricacy of the restoration procedure. Rapid and trouble-free repair completion can be facilitated by the easy accessibility of critical components. On the contrary, repair tasks become more challenging and time-intensive when components are situated in confined or inaccessible regions.
- **Availability of Technical Documentation:** The repair process can be significantly facilitated by the availability of extensive technical documentation, which may comprise service manuals, schematics, and troubleshooting guides. When maintenance staff have access to comprehensive documentation that offers guidance on diagnosing flaws and carrying out repairs efficiently, the complexity of repairs is frequently diminished.
- **Resources Required**: The skill level and expertise of maintenance professionals have a direct impact on the difficulty of repairs. Highly experienced professionals with specific training and expertise may be more suited to handling difficult repair tasks efficiently. Conversely, untrained or badly qualified people may struggle to address difficult difficulties, increasing the overall complexity of repairs.

Overall, repair complexity in machine tools is a complicated term driven by a variety of elements such as the nature of the problem, component accessibility, technical documentation availability, maintenance personnel skill level, and resource requirements. Understanding and measuring these aspects allows firms to better manage repair procedures, reduce downtime, and improve equipment reliability.

5.8 Maintenance manual

A maintenance manual for machine tools is a thorough document issued by the manufacturer to guide users, technicians, and maintenance professionals through the correct care, maintenance, and troubleshooting of a specific machine tool. These manuals are invaluable resources, precisely prepared to provide users with the knowledge and instructions required to ensure the equipment's peak performance, longevity, and safety. The Fundamental Elements of a Maintenance Manual are,

1. **Introduction:** The manual usually starts with an introduction that explains its objective, scope, and target audience. This section may also offer a summary of the machine tool, highlighting its main characteristics and uses.
2. **Safety precautions:** The incorporation of safety precautions and instructions into any maintenance handbook is an essential component that must be there in order to guarantee the health and safety of staff. Within this section, possible risks that are related with maintenance chores are brought to light, and recommendations for reducing those dangers are provided.
3. **Procedures for preventive maintenance:** For the purpose of completing routine preventive maintenance tasks, such as lubrication, cleaning, inspection, and calibration, detailed instructions are supplied. It is imperative that these procedures be followed in order to avoid early wear, preserve accuracy, and make the most of the machine tool's lifespan.
4. **Troubleshooting guidelines:** A comprehensive set of troubleshooting techniques is included in the handbook, which is designed to assist users in identifying and resolving common problems or malfunctions that may occur while the machine is being operated. The purpose of this section is to assist in the process of problem-solving by providing flowcharts, checklists, or troubleshooting trees.
5. **Repair and replacement of parts:** The manual includes detailed instructions that can be followed in order to replace or repair particular machine tool components in the event that a component fails or is damaged. Disassembly, reassembly, adjustment, and alignment techniques, as well as recommendations for spare parts, are all included in this.
6. **Maintenance schedule:** Users can plan and schedule routine maintenance tasks with the help of the offered recommended schedules and intervals. Maintenance is done proactively when following these schedules, which minimizes downtime and maximizes equipment performance.
7. **Technical specifications:** The user is provided with comprehensive technical specifications, diagrams, and schematics of the machine tool components in order to facilitate their comprehension of the machine's functioning and configuration responsibilities. This information is necessary for precisely identifying problems and carrying out maintenance in an efficient manner.

8. **Maintenance records:** Provisions for maintaining maintenance records may be included in certain manuals. These provisions could enable users to document maintenance activities, dates, tasks accomplished, as well as any observations or problems that may have been encountered. The machine tool's maintenance history may be tracked with the use of this documentation, which also assists in identifying patterns or problems that keep occurring.

Finally, a machine tool maintenance manual helps users maintain, diagnose, and optimize their equipment. Operators and maintenance staff can maximize productivity and minimize downtime by following the manual's guidelines and procedures to maintain machine tool reliability, longevity, and safety. Thus, the maintenance manual is crucial for machine tool maintenance management.

5.9 Maintenance records

Maintenance records in machine tools are detailed documentation which records all maintenance actions carried out on a specific machine tool during its operational lifecycle. These records are essential for monitoring equipment maintenance history, assessing equipment health, and making educated decisions about maintenance practices and future investments. Maintenance records usually contain the following details:

- **Date and time:** When each maintenance activity or inspection was carried out, including the date and time of the event. This assists in the establishment of a chronological record of the activities related to maintenance.
- **Maintenance task:** A description of the particular maintenance task that was carried out, which may include lubrication, cleaning, inspection, calibration, component repair, or replacement.
- **Task details:** Information about the maintenance task, such as the particular components or systems that are being maintained, the tools or equipment that are being utilized, and any observations or discoveries that were made while the maintenance activity was being carried out.
- **Technician or operator:** Identification of the technician or operator who is responsible for carrying out the maintenance task, including their name or identification. It is easier to assign responsibility and keep track of the persons who are participating in maintenance operations when this is done.
- **Duration:** The amount of time needed to finish the repair job. This gives information about how well maintenance methods work and helps plan when to do future maintenance tasks.
- **Condition assessment:** Any evaluations or assessments of the machine tool's state that were done during the maintenance task, such as notes on wear, damage, abnormalities, or signs of possible problems.

- **Maintenance Recommendations:** Recommendations or follow-up activities that are a result of the maintenance activity, such as extra repairs, changes, or additional inspections that are required to solve the issues that were detected.
- **Parts and materials used:** The records of any components, materials, lubricants, or consumables that were utilized in the course of the maintenance task, including the part numbers, quantities, and suppliers of those components.
- **Equipment calibration:** Documentation of equipment calibration conducted during maintenance, detailing calibration dates, results, and any modifications made.
- **Signature and approvals:** Signatures or permissions from authorized people are required to verify the performance of maintenance tasks and ensure compliance with maintenance processes and standards.

Organizations are able to do the following by keeping meticulous records of their maintenance activities:

- Keep a record of the maintenance history of machine tools, including the frequency, nature, and results of the tasks assigned to maintenance.
- Determine whether there are any reoccurring problems or regions that require frequent maintenance, as well as any trends or patterns in the operation of the machine.
- The duties of preventative maintenance should be scheduled more effectively based on previous data and the amount of time the equipment is used.
- Provide verification that you are in complying with the regulatory requirements, industry standards, and recommendations presented by the manufacturer.
- It is important to provide a documented history of maintenance operations and observations in order to facilitate troubleshooting and identification of problems.

In general, maintenance records are necessary for optimizing the performance, reliability, andlongevi ty of machine tools. This is because they enable organizations to make decesion basedon facts and en sure the efficient management of maintenance activities.

5.10 Housekeeping

When it comes to industry, especially when it comes to machine tools, the word "housekeeping" is very important. In this case, "housekeeping" refers to the cleaning and repair tasks that are necessary for machine tools to work well and safely. Housekeeping may not seem important when compared to the complicated workings of machines, but not doing it can have significant impacts on quality, efficiency, and, most importantly, worker safety.

At first look, it might not seem important to keep the work area clean in a situation where machines are being used. But when you look more closely, the justification is clear. Precision gears, delicate spindles, complex control panels, and rough cutting tools are just a few of the complicated parts that make up a standard machine tool. It is possible for alien objects, coolant residues, and general mess to damage all of these parts. For example, managing chips and coolant well is an important part of cleaning. Chips that build up not only make it harder for machines to work smoothly, but they can also be dangerous for people and machines. Also, coolant pools that don't move can become breeding grounds for bacteria and fungi, which can harm both the coolant and the workers' health. To maintain the highest standards of cleanliness in a machining setting, you need to adhere to these basic steps:

- **Regular cleaning schedules:** Implementing regular cleaning programs guarantees the timely elimination of contaminants and debris from machine surfaces. The implementation of this method serves to reduce the possibility of component damage and decrease the chance of flaws in machined parts that are caused by contamination.
- **Chip management:** The successful implementation of chip management systems necessitates the prompt elimination of chips that are produced during machining processes. This not only minimizes the accumulation of chips within the machine but also decreases the probability of chips being caught in moving parts, therefore avoiding expensive periods of inactivity and equipment harm
- **Maintenance of coolant:** The meticulous upkeep of coolant systems is vital in order to uphold the efficacy of coolant and extend the lifespan of tools. Consistently monitoring the concentration of coolant, pH levels, and microbiological contamination helps to prevent problems that may negatively impact machining performance.
- **Storage and evaluation of tools:** The examination of cutting tools for signs of wear and damage, as well as their proper storage when not in use, are essential elements of maintaining cleanliness and orderliness. The implementation of appropriate tool maintenance practices is crucial in maintaining constant machining accuracy and extending the lifespan of tools, hence leading to improved productivity and cost reduction.
- **Workpiece organization:** Ensuring a workspace free from clutter enhances operating efficiency and reduces the possibility of accidents. The implementation of well-defined pathways and specifically designated storage places for equipment and materials serves to optimize workflow efficiency and expedite the retrieval of essential resources.

In summary, housekeeping in machine tools is more than just tidiness; it represents a proactive approach to maintaining equipment integrity, optimizing machining performance, and ensuring worker safety. Manufacturers may maintain operational excellence as well as the highest quality and safety standards by focusing on cleanliness and maintenance in machining settings.

5.11 Total productive maintenance

Total Productive Maintenance (TPM) is a comprehensive methodology for the maintenance and management of equipment that emerged in Japan and has since gained significant recognition in the global manufacturing industry. In the context of machine tools, TPM specifically pertains to the implementation of TPM principles and practices. Machine tools are essential assets in manufacturing operations, and it is imperative to maximize their uptime and productivity to achieve optimal operational efficiency. TPM in machine tools emphasizes proactive maintenance strategies, involving both operators and maintenance personnel, to ensure the equipment's optimal performance, reliability, and longevity.

The use of TPM concepts in the context of machine tools is as follows:

1. **Autonomous maintenance (AM)**
    - Operators are provided with training and authority to carry out regular maintenance duties on the machine tools, including but not limited to cleaning, lubrication, inspection, and small adjustments.
    - The primary objective of Asset Management (AM) is to mitigate the degradation of machine conditions, promptly detect any irregularities, and ensure that equipment remains in an optimal operational state.
    - By actively engaging operators in the maintenance process, machine tools are effectively maintained, resulting in enhanced reliability and decreased periods of inactivity.
2. **Planned maintenance (PM)**
    - PM is the process of planning regular maintenance tasks based on how the machines are used and their state.
    - Some repairs are aligning, calibrating, replacing worn parts, and planning maintenance based on monitoring the health of the equipment.
    - If maintenance is done ahead of time, unexpected breakdowns are less likely to happen and the machines last longer generally.
3. **Quality maintenance (QM)**
    - In quality management, the primary focus is on ensuring that machine tools consistently deliver items of a high quality.
    - This involves fixing any problems that may arise with the machine's accuracy, repeatability, and stability, all of which have the potential to impact the quality of the product.
    - It is possible to eliminate variances in product quality that are caused by equipment-related issues by ensuring that machine tools are kept in optimal condition. This, in turn, leads to an improvement in the overall quality of the product.

4. Training and education

- It is vital for both operators and maintenance people to participate in appropriate training and education programs in order to ensure that they possess the information and abilities necessary to accurately carry out their respective tasks.
- Training may cover topics such as technique for troubleshooting, maintenance processes, safety protocols, and the functioning of various pieces of equipment.
- Employees who have received enough training are in a better position to recognize possible problems at an earlier stage, carry out maintenance activities in the appropriate manner, and contribute to the overall success of TPM programs.

5. Early equipment management (EEM)

- During the phases of design, procurement, and installation of new machine tools, EEM requires taking into consideration the maintenance requirements that are necessary.
- It is possible to lower overall life cycle costs and maintenance requirements by selecting equipment that has a high level of maintainability, reliability, and ease of serviceability.
- Furthermore, using the appropriate processes for installation and commissioning ensures that the machine tools get off to a good start, hence reducing the number of problems that arise while they are in operation.

It is necessary to follow a methodical approach, have strong backing from leadership, and have active engagement from all stakeholders in order to successfully implement TPM in machine tools. Organizations have the ability to achieve higher equipment reliability, decreased downtime, enhanced product quality, and ultimately increased productivity and competitiveness in the manufacturing industry by implementing the principles of Total Productive Maintenance (TPM).

KNOW MORE

SPM and Maintenance of Machine Tools

SUMMARY

This Chapter includes information about special purpose machines (SPMs) are custom-designed machines aimed at specific tasks to enhance productivity. They consist of general elements like specialized tools, fixtures, and automation systems, designed with principles focusing on efficiency and precision. In machine tool maintenance, various types include preventive, predictive, and corrective maintenance, supported by repair cycle analysis and repair complexity evaluation. Maintenance manuals, records, and good housekeeping practices are essential for effective upkeep. Total Productive Maintenance (TPM) integrates maintenance into daily operations, emphasizing proactive and preventive strategies to maximize machine reliability and efficiency.

EXERCISE

1. Explain the General elements of the special-purpose machine.
2. Explain the principles of SPM design.
3. Explain in detail the types of maintenance.
4. Write different steps involved in repair cycle analysis.
5. Write details of maintenance records.
6. Short note on:

   I. Housekeeping

   II. TPM

REFERENCES

1. B. W. Charman (1968), Special Purpose Production Machines, Harper Collins Distribution Services, ISBN: 0258967382, Page: 1-120.
2. M.M. Dole (2018), Mechanic Machine Tool Maintenance Training, Papyrus.

BIBLIOGRAPHY

Begman, M.L., and Amsted, B.H., Manufacturing Processes, John Willey and Sons, 6th Edition, (1969).

Bohez, E.L.J. (2002) Five-axis milling machine tool kinematic chain design and analysis, International Journal of Machine Tools & Manufacture, **42** (2002) 505–520.

Davim, J.P. Nontraditional Machining Processes: Research Advances, 1st edition, Chapter 4, UK: Springer-Verlag, 2013.

Dewangan, S. K. (2010) Experimental Investigation of Machining Parameters for EDM using U-shaped Electrode of AISI P20 Tool Steel, eThesis, NIT Rourkela.

Ghodsiyeh, D. (2013). Review on Current Research Trends in Wire Electrical Discharge Machining (WEDM). Indian Journal of Science and Technology, 6(2), 1–15. https://doi.org/10.17485/ijst/2013/v6i2.18.

Ghosh, A. and Mallick, A.K. Manufacturing Science, 2nd edition, East-West Press (India) Pvt Ltd, 2010.

Goetsch, D.L., Advanced manufacturing technology, Delmar Publisher, (1990).

Jain, V.K. Advanced manufacturing process, (2009).

Joshi, P.H. Jigs and Fixtures, 3rd edition, Tata McGraw Hill, (2010).

Kalpakjian, S. and Schmid, S.R., Manufacturing Engineering and Technology (SI Edition), 7th edition, Pearson Education (2018).

Koc, M. and Ozel, T. Micro-Manufacturing: Design and Manufacturing of Micro-Products, 1st edition, Chapter 10, USA: John Willey and Sons, 2011.

Krar, S.F. and Gil, A., Exploring Advanced Manufacturing Technologies, Industrial Press, (2003).

Kumar, S., Singh, R., Singh, T.P. and Sethi, B.L. (2009) Surface modification by electrical discharge machining: a review. Journal of Materials Processing Technology, **209** (8), 3675-3687.

Kunieda, M., Lauwers, B., Rajurkar, K.P. and Schumacher, B.M. (2005) Advancing EDM through fundamental insight into the process. CIRP Annals - Manufacturing Technology, **54** (2), 64-87.

Mistha, P.K., Non-conventional Machining, Narvasa Publishing House (2018).

Pabla, B.S and Adithan, M., CNC machines, New Age International Limited, (2008).

Payal, H.S. and Sethi, B.L. (2003) Non-conventional machining processes as viable alternatives for production with specific reference to electrical discharge machining. Journal of Scientific and Industrial Research, **62**, 678-682.

Production Technology – HMT, Banglore, Tata Mc-Graw Hill.

Raghuwanshi, B.S., Workshop Technology, Vol II, Dhanpat Rai and Co, (2015).

Sathishkumar, R., Swaminathan, S., Sena, M., Dinakaran, P.T., (2017) Design and development of special purpose machine using hydro-pneumatic cylinders to do 4 holes and 2 holes piercing in a square tube", International Journal of Mechanical Engineering and Technology (IJMET), Volume 8, Issue 3, 209-218.

Takahata, K. Micro Electronic and Mechanical Systems, 1st edition, Chapter 10, Croatia: INTECH, 2009.

APPENDICES

Appendix-A

PLC Programming for Industrial Automation

Appendix-B

A Case Study On Manufacturing Industry Used Prognostic Tools To Remove The Problems In Shop Floor Challenges Faced In Maintenance Engineering.

CO AND PO ATTAINMENT TABLE

Course outcomes (COs) for this course can be mapped with the program outcomes (POs) after the completion of the course and a correlation can be made for the attainment of POs to analyze the gap. After proper analysis of the gap in the attainment of POs necessary measures can be taken to overcome the gaps.

Table for CO and PO attainment

Course Outcomes	Attainment of Programme Outcomes *(1- Weak Correlation; 2- Medium correlation; 3- Strong Correlation)*						
	PO-1	**PO-2**	**PO-3**	**PO-4**	**PO-5**	**PO-6**	**PO-7**
CO-1							
CO-2							
CO-3							
CO-4							
CO-5							

The data filled in the above table can be used for gap analysis.

INDEX

Adjustable Vee locator 10
Applications of jig boring machine 32
Applications of plastics 47
Application of EDM 67
Applications of wire EDM 73
Abrasive water-jet machining (AWJM) 73
Automatic tool changer and magazine 91
Programming methods 94
Type of controller 95
Box Jig 4
Basic principle of location 6
Boring fixture 16
Blow moulding 43
Block Diagram of PLC 118
Cylindrical locators 8
Cam operated clamp 19
Compression Moulding 38
Casting 42
Calendering 43
Control process parameter of wire EDM 71
Classification of machining centers 89
Control System Machine Tool System 92
Common preparatory function (G- codes) 97
Common Miscellaneous Function (M- codes) 101
Canned Cycle 102
Drill bushes 10
Double-column jig boring machine 30
Direct blow moulding 43
Description of EDM equipment 60
Extrusion 41
Electrical discharge machining 57
EDM process parameter 64
Electrochemical machining 82

Elements of control system 109
Forming and shaping of plastics 35
Fixed V-locator 9
Flash mould 40
Grinding fixtures 16
General elements of special purpose machine 124
Headed bush 11
Hydraulic clamping 22
Housekeeping 136
Indexing jig 6
Important consideration in clamp design 17
Introduction jig boring 26
Indirect blow moulding 44
Injection Moulding 37
Jig Boring 26
Leaf Jig 3
Locating methods and devices 8
Long bush in two section 12
Leadscrew Method 32
Lamination and reinforcement 44
Laminates 44
Laminated tube and rods 46
Low pressure laminating 46
Laser beam machining 80
Limit switches 111
Milling fixtures 13
Methods of locating holes in jig boring 31
Mechanical and electrical gauging method 32
Moulding 33
Machine tool automation 104
Maintenance of Machine Tools 128
Maintenance manual 133
Maintenance records 134
Optical measuring method 32
Output characteristics of EDM 66

Plate jig 5
Plain bush 10
Pneumatic clamping 23
Plastics 47
Processing of plastics 36
Principles of computer-aided part programming 103
Proximity switches 114
Programmable Logic Controller (PLC) 117
Productivity Improvement by SPM 125
Principles of SPM 126
Repair cycle analysis 130
Repair complexity 132
Strap clamp 18
Screw clamp 20
Single-column jig boring 30
Steps in moulding 33
Semi-positive compression moulding 40
Subroutine 102
Single spindle automates 106
Servo Control System 116
Types of Jig 3
Template Jig 5
Toggle clamp 22
Types of jig boring 29
Thermoplastic plastics 34
Thermosetting plastics 34
Transfer moulding 41
Tool magazine 92
Transfer lines 107
Total productive maintenance 137
Universal Jig 6
Ultrasonic machining 54
Vice fixture 12
Wedge clamp 21
Wire electric discharge machining 68